# 1812 And all That

**Sound And Vision**

# 1812 And all That

## A Concise History of Music from 30.000 BC to the Millennium

## Lawrence Leonard

**Sound And Vision**

# – About the Author –

I first met Lawrence Leonard when he was an undistinguished cellist on the back desk of the London Philharmonic Orchestra.

I was, at the time, first trumpet.

Later, Lawrence became an equally undistinguished conductor who was lucky enough to be employed in such centres of culture as Mid-West Canada, East Germany, Turkey, Yugoslavia, South Africa and Luxembourg. During these years he wrote several arrangements which have yet to be performed, one of these being the *Grande Messe de Notre Dame* of Guillaume de Machaut, a work that happened to be out of copyright at the time.

It is indeed fortunate that Lawrence Leonard has found, in this book and at his advanced age, a suitable receptacle for his talents, such as they may be.

*Sir Malcolm Arnold, CBE*

The days when Lawrence Leonard and I used to walk over Boxhill together are thankfully over, days that were somewhat hampered by Lawrence's apparent inability to walk and talk at the same time.

In spite of this and the many other disadvantages from which he suffers, my admiration for a man who can make the Webern *Orchestral Variations* last 10 minutes longer than scheduled remains unclouded.

His work on the Ordnance Survey map of Surrey during which he manages to locate Dorking a little to the East of Notting Hill Gate deserves special mention.

*John Amis*

Lawrence Leonard has been known to me for some years as the slowest conductor in Europe. He once managed to add an hour to a performance of the *The Marriage of Figaro,* a feat that I would have thought impossible. It is well known that his standard performance of *Messiah* lasts over two evenings largely so that he can perform *How beautiful are the feet* at a tempo which he feels sufficiently expressive, and his well-known attempts to perform Beethoven's symphonies at Beethoven's metronome markings have led to the mental deterioration from which he has not yet completely recovered.

*Sir Charles Mackerras*

# – Table of Contents –

## – A Preamble –

A chronological Map of World Music before Christ.

30,000 BC: Rhodesian Man and his bone hunting-horns

25,000 BC: Java Man and his bone nose-flutes.

20,000 BC: Peking Man and his bone bongo drums.

15,000 BC: Heidelberg Man and his bone castanets (?)

10,000 BC: Piltdown Man and his legendary tuned skulls (?)

5,000 BC:  The Aegeans and their untuned vocalizing.

1,000 BC:  Greece.

700 BC:    The Pythic Gnome.

600 BC:    Archilochus and his trochee.

550 BC:    The Dyonisiac Agony.

500 BC:    The theoretical works of Aristoxenus of Tarentum.

000 AD:    Jesus Christ.

Now read on.

# – Chapter 1 –

## Primitive Music

How did music begin?

To discover this, we must resort to the Theory of Extrapolation. Although this may not describe precisely how Early Man behaved in the Mediterranean Basin, there is always the chance it may.

First, find a baby and excite its emotions (take away breast, make funny faces, bark like a seal). The resultant sound is primitive melody that reached its apogee in the songs of Schubert and Rodgers and Hart, to name but three.

Now find another baby and see if you can make it stamp its feet, hit saucepans etc. If you can, you have before you an example of primitive rhythm as exemplified in the works of Xenakis, Stravinsky and Carl Orff, who was so affected by the sound of the saucepans that he shouted an expletive so explosive he later adopted it as his professional name. Not much is known about Xenackys due to the impossibility of spelling or pronouncing his name.

At this point, some of you may ask: "What about Fixed Tonal Centres and Sprung Meters?" If you do, the reply must be in the negative. (*Strukturprobleme in Primitiver Musick*, Steinitz, 1931).

If, however, you have a question about phrase structure in the last 10 bars of *The Rite of Spring*, we cannot do better than point you in the direction of *How to Stabilize Unequal Metres,* issued in 1963 by the N. Thames Gas Board (pamphlet No:3A).

### The Greeks

Apart from Ur, Urtext, and a few other Middle Eastern civilizations too problematic to mention, the first proper music came from Greece, but as it was used mainly to accompany dance it wasn't listened to very carefully (see Ballet).

Greek music also played a major role in the theatre (where it was known as *The Greek Tragedy*), although no one is sure what it was. Stravinsky, who wrote the music for *Odious Rex,* knew, but refused to say.

He did, however, have the work translated into French so he could understand it and give it a 'timeless quality,' and so well did he succeed that his version has since been translated back into Greek for its annual performances in the Parthenon Room of the British Museum.

The whole question of what instruments the Greeks used is still shrouded in mystery – it will be remembered that the infant Hermes killed a turtle and fastened on its shell the strings from the entrails of an ox. But it is less certain if, when Orpheus dropped his lyre into the sea, it drifted to the isle of Lesbos, where Hyagnis and Marsyas were busy inventing the aulus.

From this explosive situation arose the traditional conflict between the lyre and the aulus, which was to remain unresolved throughout Greek history, except possibly by the Greeks themselves.

We do know, however, that all Greek music was written on the white notes of the harp, each one of which was a Mode or Column (Ionian, Corinthian,

Dorian, etc.), and that the ladies playing them (Harpies) posed for several million Greek vases, most of which are now in The Vatican Museum (Room CVXIII)

At one time, the Greeks also played flutes, but Socrates put a stop to it. This was because it might give children lascivious thoughts about double-tonguing, etc.

Apart from the fact that the Harpies kept getting their Modes/Columns mixed up (Mixolydian), little more is known about Greek music since the two most extensive examples ever discovered were written on a stone, since lost.

### The Byzantines

The Byzantines had no lyres or auli, but they had organs they used to great effect, hiding them inside stone lions. As theatres and pantomimes had both been banned by the Laodicean Council, all that was left were Ceremonies, both religious and secular.

These Ceremonies were occasions of the greatest excitement, largely because the Byzantines used to hide their choirs behind curtains. This was said to be intensely dramatic and awe-inspiring, especially as they used to sing in Emphases in which only accented syllables were recognized as 'long'. The emotional effect of this system often led to ladies fainting through hyperventilation.

### The Romans

The Romans, who imitated the Greeks whenever they could, had the two pieces of stone referred to above copied out and passed over to a piccolo player called Ottorino Resphigi to arrange for large orchestra so they could be played at or under the various Fountains, Pine Trees and Festivals of Rome.

As is well known, the Romans were predominantly a military race, much given to war and if possible conquest, and for this they needed brass instruments to play fanfares (Bucinas, Tuba Mirums and Strumpets).

So effective were these instruments in battle that they were later mass produced by Boosey and Hawkes and sold to military bands all over the Roman Empire, so they could be played at special brass band competitions at which the Emperor himself would signify the winner or otherwise by a gesture of the thumb. This is generally recognized as the beginning of Music Criticism as we know it.

*The Others*

These include Babylon, Judea, the Euphrates Basin, The Empty Quarter and the Far East.

In Islamic countries, most music was strongly influenced by the chants of the Muezzin – but in the others, not so much.

In Babylon, Sung Evensong usually took place on either side of the Waters, with the choristers on one side and the congregation on the other, weeping.

In Judea, professionals wailers were often employed to express miserable thoughts at the Wailing Wall, as members of the public were allowed only five minutes per wail. If their feelings had not been properly expressed by then, they would pay for a Wailer to express them for them.

The Empty Quarter had the usual indigenous collection of reed instruments, but as there was no one to listen to them, music as a Communication Art became non-existent.

The Euphrates Basin and Mesopotamia also had little in the way of significant art forms of their own, although it is believed the Tower of Babel served as a repository for many Museum Cultures that might otherwise have been lost.

There was little doubt, however, that the Top Musical Nation of the Ancient World was Egypt, who produced large orchestras of flutes, lyres and drums to play to the many visitors at Luxor and the Aswan Damn.

As for the Indian sub-continent, Polynesia and the Far East, none of our regular contributors were prepared to hazard a guess, although some are currently engaged in preparing a paper based on evidence from some of the better restaurants in the Manchester area.

*Review I*

Which is your baby best at: Melody or Rhythm?

Can you tell the difference between the songs of Rodgers and Hart?

Have you heard of Schubert and if so, where?

Name two Greek vases

Who played the reed instruments in the Empty Quarter? Why?

Where are the Waters of Babylon and who wrote it?

*Review 1* continued

Write a short piece in the style of the Euphrates Basin.

Hide a choir behind a curtain.

Arrange a Festival in Rome, for large orchestra, and ask them what they would like to drink.

Was Resphigi a type of fungus?

## – Chapter 2 –

*Folk Music* (Hungary and Norfolk)

Folk Music began when the Dark Ages set in (early nights, etc.), especially in Hungary and Norfolk. As it was too dark to read, it was essentially an Oral Tradition (see Oral Training) but one fragment exists, discovered recently under a Norfolk broad:

*Thee thyme hass cum thee Woll*
*Rhoss sed too speke orff meni thinges.*
*Orff shuse end shippes end seel in whacks*
*Orff cebb edges end kinges.*

(Cecil Sharp surmises that this fragment could have been sung to the tune of *Cum amollocking next Tuesday.*)

In Hungary, all folk songs were in 7/8 or 5/8 time to distinguish them from the Norfolk ones, but as they all had names like *Bagy* or *Szekely Rashnya*, people did not often refer to them.

Whereas Cecil Sharp, Vaughan Williams and Holst used to spend their summers going round the pubs of Norfolk persuading the locals to sing something for the price of a half of mild, Bartok and Kodaly never got away with less than a bottle of Slivovitz, which accounted for most of the five- and seven-eights.

Although this sort of nonsense was acceptable enough in Norfolk and Budapest, it wasn't good enough for the Germans, who decided the whole folksong business should be better organized.

With this in mind, they founded a proper guild of very small singers, called Minnesingers, and made them go round the country holding singing competitions in the open air. These were such a success that they raised the standards of *Eisteddfodds* and similar religious festivals throughout the Western world. Because these competitions were all sung in Old German, which had a funny alphabet that no one could understand except the Welsh, large numbers of Welsh cottages were later bought up by Germans for use as holiday homes.

Meanwhile the French, having heard about the *Minnesingers*, engaged the services of a fictitious singer called Roland and told him to invent the French *chanson*, which he did.

The success made of these *chansons* by later singers such as Edith Piaf and Simone de Beauvoir led to the foundation of a group called The Existentialists, which was responsible for many of the student riots in Paris during the 1960s.

Jean Cocteau, who played drums in the group, later made a film called *Orphee* in which he attempted to show that the French *chanson* had been invented by the Greeks (see Stravinsky), but he was unable to substantiate this and Roland was reinstated in 1968.

*Folk music* (Others)

There is little doubt that folk songs existed in other parts of the world, such as Istanbul, Oban and The Empty Quarter, but as no one collected any of them, they were just left lying around. However, a UNESCO committee, chaired by Bob Dylan, has recently been travelling round the world picking them up and as a result, *I'll tak the High Road* and *Egeshagara, Bayan* have both been elevated to genuine folksong status, as has *Je regret rien* and *We love you, Princess.*

It is hoped that more material will be forthcoming from this committee when it has completed its tour of The Empty Quarter scheduled for the Millennium.

*Church Music*

As can be imagined, none of this stuff was very suitable for Church use, especially Roland, so Pope Gregory or Bishop Ambrose invented Gregorian or Ambrosian plainsong to give the monks something more appropriate to sing.

This meant sorting out the Greek modes, which the Harpies had left in a dreadful mess. For this task they chose Boethius, who claimed he had once met Ptolemy and thus knew a good deal about them. In spite of this, he still got them wrong, although everyone pretended not to notice.

The trouble with plainsong was that, as the piano had not yet been invented nor had chords, the monks had to sing everything in unison. This sounded so appallingly dull that Pope Gregory or Ambrose made them all go to Solesme, which was near the famous motor-racing track at Le Mans, to find a way of making it more lively.

After some years of hard work, they said they had now invented *organum*, in which half the monks sang a fifth lower than the others, and could they come back? Alas, the popes still found it too dull and said they must stay where they were and keep trying.

This they did, finally coming up with the hocket, which called for some of the singers to sing everything a little after everyone else. This was judged a great improvement, but by then the monks were so fed up with the popes that they didn't tell them about it but sent the idea straight off to the Netherlands, where it was greeted with enthusiasm by the Flemish School and much developed by such composers as Okeghem, Hockeysticks and Hoquenheim.

Shortly after this, the organ was invented and composers were allowed proper names such as Palestrina. This was of great help to the popes when they wanted to send out a bull, which they did with increasing frequency once they realized polyphony had been invented without their noticing, and that some composers were taking advantage by writing too many parts and putting rude songs in the bass. (*La Belle Dame sans Merci*, etc.)

The result of this was to obscure the words of the liturgy, which it was essential should be heard, so the popes told the singers to enunciate the words of the liturgy very clearly and the words of the rude songs very badly. At this, the congregations complained they couldn't hear the words of the rude songs any more, so the popes punished them by getting the liturgy put in the bass and the rude songs on top, where there were so many parts imitating each other they couldn't be heard at all.

The congregations therefore complained again, so the popes had large wooden screens erected between them and the singers so they couldn't hear anything except echo. This also enabled the choristers to get away with dirty surplices and having a nap during sermons.

It was about this time that England became highly regarded as a musical nation because the country had a real Queen at last and everyone wanted to do their best for her by joining the Chapel Royal and writing Catholic or Protestant Masses so she could decide which she liked best. England also had the best composers in Europe.

*Review II*

Who was it that was discovered under a Norfolk broad?

Exactly where is Hungary?

How many half-pints of mild ale did it take to make Holst drunk?

Did Bartok ever meet Cecil Sharp? Why not?

Who was the lead singer of The Existentialists?

Why was Roland fictitious?

What was the upper height limit of a Minnesinger?

Were Gregory and Ambrose the same person and what was their name?

What is your opinion, if any, of a Hocket? Where would you put a rude song?

# – Chapter 3 –

## The Madrigalists

If people wanted a bit of entertainment outside church and didn't live in Norfolk, they would sing madrigals sitting round a table. This was amateur musicmaking at its best because if someone went wrong, all that happened was the others would laugh and say things like: "You help him out, Joan."

The best madrigals were written by the English because of their sense of humor and gift for double meanings. Thus, if they sang about Death it was understood they had just made love and if they sang about roses it meant ladies' lips or worse.

If one of the singers didn't want to sing words like these or couldn't see them because they were on the wrong side of the table, they would pick up a block-flute or something similar and play the notes on that. This was called a Broken Concert and was usually a signal for everyone to get up and go home, if possible with Joan.

Madrigals were not only an English art form. Isaac the German wrote some for Italy, Josquin the Netherlander wrote them for the French and Lechner the Austrian wrote them for Germany.

Large transfer fees were paid for composers such as these to work in foreign lands, but even so they never seemed able to compose as well as the English, so in order to overcome this inability, some of them thought it might be a good idea to string several madrigals together so that they told a story.

## The Beginnings of Opera

As soon as he heard about this invention, Monty Verdi, a distant relative of Giuseppe, realized it could easily get out of hand, so in 1607 he invented an opera.

This he called *Orfeo* and he cleverly scored it for a collection of very out-of-date instruments no one had ever heard of so later musicians could adapt it to modern resources, thus keeping the work permanently in the repertoire.

Once someone has a good idea, everyone starts copying it.

Soon, anyone with a theatre to his or her name was commissioning an opera to put in it. It was easy to see why *Orfeo* was such a favorite because of the romance between Orfeo and Euridice and because of the lyre and the mirror, and lots of composers tried their hand at it. There were even several operas called *Euridice*, giving her side of the story, and one called *The Lyre and Mirror,* which everyone thought was about a tavern.

Of the many other subjects illuminated by this new art form were *Antiparnassus, Aspidestra, Acton and Diana* and *The Desperation of Filharmonia.*

As soon as it was realized this invention was going to be a success, an enterprising section of the Musician's Union announced "that old music can be performed only on old instruments."

This was directly opposed to Monty Verdi's theories, but as soon as the profession realized how many jobs this new decision would create, what with new workshops in which to make the old instruments and musicologists to tell everyone what they ought to sound like, it was proposed and seconded at an extraordinary meeting of the Royal Society and passed *nem.con.*

Shawms began to take the place of oboes, recorders were elevated to *flutes-a-bec* and all the strings began playing on gut strings. Unfortunately, the genuine 17th century string instruments already in use in modern symphony orchestras were unavailable, so imitations had to be made by Yamaha.

The success of the new art form was such that everyone in Europe began practising it except the English, who persuaded Dr. Johnson to announce that opera was an exotic and irrational entertainment and then engaged Charles Dibden, the composer, playwright, poet and novelist, to write a series of operettas to prove that it was.

However...

### Henry Purcell

Realizing that Purcell was the last great English composer until Elgar, the English decided to make an exception in his case. This was very good of them as they were busy restoring the monarchy at the time and what they really needed were masques, or masks.

Purcell chose as his subject "When I am laid in earth," and composed it entirely on a ground bass. It was a great success and ran for one night at Josias Priest's Boarding School for Young Ladies, Chelsea, in 1689.

Purcell also wrote a piece in which the viola (or tenor viol, as it was then called) played the same note all the way through, so Benjamin Britten could record it later. Britten also popularized a theme of Henry Purcell's by writing some variations on it, and generally helped the composer to achieve recognition by editing a lot of his music.

Many other musicians also contributed to Purcell's reputation by arranging suites from his operas and scoring them for strings played entirely in the first position, with fingerings and bowings marked in. These were found to be ideal for performance in schools or in amateur string orchestras up and down the country.

In Europe, Purcell was regarded with some suspicion when it was discovered he was neither Shakespeare nor of German nor Italian descent.

## The Rise of Germany as Top Musical Nation

The seeds of this rise were sown by Martin Luther, the well known lutenist. Finding the Roman Catholic habit of using choirs of small boys singing behind screens both secretive and undemocratic, Luther decided to invent the Protestant church.

He did this by translating the Latin liturgy into German so everyone could understand it, and then by writing some very simple tunes the whole congregation could sing if the organ played a little in front all the time.

These tunes were called chorales and they were a great inspiration to all. They led not only to Bach, Mozart and Beethoven, but to the English hymnal as well.

How did this happen?

### Review III

Say what you mean by Death and then write a short madrigal.

Who was Joan and what was her function?

Could you find a ground bass if you were told where to look?

Was Martin Luther a prig?

25

*Review III* continued

Why was Purcell named after a brand of soap powder?

Which was the one note Purcell wrote for Britten to play?

Name the last school at which you heard one of Purcell's Suites attempted.

Write a Chorale and put some German words to it.

Was Charles Dibden as popular as Gilbert and Sullivan, and why not?

## – Chapter 4 –

### Johann Sebastian Bach

J.S. Bach, as he was jocularly known to his friends, got so fed up with playing a bit in front all the time that he determined to put a stop to it. He did this by writing Moving Parts, thus forcing the congregation to keep up with him. After some years, these Moving Parts began getting a hold on him and he wrote so many of them he was was tempted to dispense with the congregation altogether and have some proper singers instead, which was not exactly what Martin Luther had had in mind.

He also found that most of the chorales Luther had collected throughout Germany were badly in need of a few moving parts and thus the *Chorale Prelude* was born. These chorales were found to be so useful as a means of teaching harmony that music colleges sprung up all over Europe so people could be taught to write it properly, first without Moving Parts and later with.

It was at about this time that Bach began getting a bit above himself in various ways, such as trying to conduct the university choir, inventing things for his second wife to do and composing a six-part fugue on Frederick the Great while he was playing the flute.

By the end of his life, it is calculated that Bach had written some 254,367,575,463 notes, mainly semiquavers, or sixteenth notes. He also wrote a book called *The Art of Fugue* but failed to finish it due to pressure of work.

No account of Bach's life would be complete without reference to his *Passions*, of which there were two, both based on Moving Parts.

Nor would it be complete without reference to his *Preludes and Fugues*, of which he wrote one of each in every key known to man, including C-sharp major. He did this, and various other things, because once he had an idea, he refused to relinquish it until he had exhausted all its possibilities. He did the same with his two marriages.

Bach also wrote six concerti for the Duke of Brandenburg, one of which had no violins for reasons that remain unclear, and six suites for unaccompanied cello, which have been responsible for more empty seats than any other pieces in the repertoire. This is not because they are not good, but because the unaccompanied cello leaves something to be desired as a vehicle for high art.

It is entirely possible Bach wrote more music to the glory of God than anyone else in the world. Certainly the Protestant Church would find it difficult to survive without him, as it would then have to play music by other composers whose names for the moment slip our memory.

### The Italian Violin School

This did not exist and it is included here only in order to expose one of the the most daring confidence tricks in the history of music.

Between 1680 and 1730, some Italians called Fake-it Amati, Fake-it Stradivarius and Fake-it Guarneri pretended they were great violin makers, whereas if you looked carefully at the label inside the violin, you could see the word *model* written underneath in very small letters, thus proving that the violins were all made by Boosey and Hawkes and came complete with bow, case and resin.

Nevertheless, a school of violin composers arose to write music for these instruments, including such apparently okay names as Vivaldi, Corelli, Vitale, Pugnani, Tartini and others.

Only in the light of 20th century research has it been revealed that these were all pseudonyms for the celebrated violinist Fritz Kreisler, who used to get so fed up practising the fiddle that he would sometimes sit down and write a couple of sonatas for violin and piano (!) in the style of the 17th century for a change.

He would then play them through to see if they were all right, and if they were, send them off to his publisher, saying he had discovered them recently in an Italian church during his last tour and they were by Vivaldi (or Corelli, Vitale, Pugnani or Tartini) and would the publisher like to publish them in this special edition he had recently made himself?

The publisher would then publish them, putting them all to his blind eye and making a dreadful vow that he would never reveal the real identity of their composer.

### Bach's Sons

Like their father, these were always referred to by their initials.

The best known were C.P.E. and J.C. and, to a lesser extent, W.F. Some say there was also a P.D.Q., but this has never been proven.

Neither C.P.E., J.C. nor W.F. was as good at Moving Parts as their father, so instead they decided to invent a new style called the Style Gallant or Gallant Style, which consisted of writing a top line and then sending it to Italy for someone called Alberti to fill in the bass and harmonies.

So successful were these compositions that the Bachs (as they were known) began ornamenting the top line with *acciaccaturas* and the like, which led to yet another style called Rococo, meaning a bit of old rockwork. (Old French: *rocaille*). J.C., who died in St. Pancras churchyard and was thus referred to as the English Bach, had a bit put over his grave.

J.S. himself, recognizing his children's talents, used to say: "No one wants to hear my music any more. My sons are writing the sort of pieces people want to hear nowadays."

There must have been some truth in this, for no one played J.S.'s music for another 200 years, until Mendlessohn decided it was time to rediscover it. So monumental did everyone then find it, they at once stopped playing Bach's sons' music and went back to the old man's.

The Protestant Church thereby recovered some of its former glory and the word Rococo suffered a decline so severe no one could remember what it meant.

Indeed, so degraded did the word become that people began making jokes about it like: "Have a slice of Baroque and a cup of Rococo?" Architects used to say buildings with too much decoration were Rococo and the word finally came to rest on the Albert Memorial.

*The English Choral Tradition*

As soon as Handel heard of J.S.'s success with Passions, Moving Parts, etc. he realized he must make his mark elsewhere, so he went to Italy to learn how to write operas. This he did pretty quickly, and on hearing that England had no decent composers now that Purcell was dead, he decided to go there and try them out.

They were a huge success, so much so that Handel nearly went bankrupt three times before the English decided to nationalize him and make him write oratorios instead. This was clever of the English for a variety of reasons.

First, the singers didn't have to dress up, except in evening clothes, which they bought themselves, nor did they have to memorize their parts. Instead, all they had to do was to learn how to turn over the pages of the score in the mood of the aria they were singing at the time, and then how to fix the audience with one eye whilst using the other to read the music.

Both of these were less demanding than trying to act. In fact, on almost every level, oratorios were cheaper than than opera: There was no scenery, no wardrobe mistresses, no stage managers, carpenters, electricians, producers or designers.

Conductors were still, unfortunately, necessary and so were orchestras, but the choirs who sang the choruses were amateurs.

This meant that oratorios gave the English something to do in the evenings apart from going to bed (Pepys). It was called choir practice, and it led to so much extra-choral activity, such as sharing the same coach home, that the authorities decided to put a stop to it, restricting the choirs to three and making them all live near Gloucester.

The English choral tradition was most upset at this, seeing the action as unnecessarily high-handed, and its members found their own ways of circumventing it by forming clandestine Glee Clubs, especially in the North. It is not known how these groups got their name, given the phlegmatic nature of their members and the nostalgic nature of their repertoire, but it may have been satire, for which most Northerners had a talent.

Handel himself became so cross at these restrictions that he gave the first performance of *Messiah* in Dublin with 283 oboes.

*Review IV*

Play any one semi-quaver of a Bach Moving Part.

What would you do if Fritz Kreisler really were Pugnani, Vitale, etc.?

Did Alberti write any tunes of his own?

Give three examples of extra-choral activity.

Think of an oratorio and then invent some scenery for it.

Turn over the pages of your music in the style of *How beautiful are the feet.*

*– Chapter 5 –*

*The Development of Opera*

Little has been said so far about the French, except Roland, but they had not been idle – they had been trying to take opera away from the Italians.

This was not easy as the English had realized when they invented the oratorio. By doing this and by bribing Dr. Johnson to express himself so strongly, they had more or less indicated they were prepared to throw in the sponge and leave it to others.

The French, however, were made of sterner stuff. Also they had the Palace of Versailles and the Sun King and they wanted some entertainments that might reflect "La Gloire de la France", as they liked to put it. This meant spending a lot of money on scenery so the audience had plenty to look at while the music was going on.

It was, of course, a well-known fact that the Italians not only discovered opera, but were best at it, so it was not surprising it was toward that country the French now looked for inspiration, sending out spies to all the big Italian operatic centres, such as Naples and Foggia, to discover whom they should engage and for how much.

As a result of these researches, they hired a Florentine called Lully, who realized immediately the reason the French couldn't write operas properly was that they couldn't understand Italian.

He put this right by writing 14 of them, all in French, and then killed himself by hitting his foot with his baton, which he then passed over to Rameau, who was four at the time, telling him to write nine more.

This Rameau did.

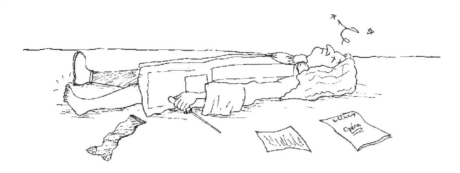

Once the Italians got wind of this, they were furious, and sent over one of their best men, Pergolesi, with an *opera buffa* called *La Serva Padrona* (She Served the Padre) and sat back to await results.

They were not long in coming. As soon as *le Douanier* Jean-Jacques Rousseau heard this work, he said, "French opera is useless," and proceeded to write one himself to prove it. It was called *Devin le Village* and it was really a pastorale about French village life. So boring was this piece that Rousseau wrote a book defending it. This rash gesture, coming from someone who was really a customs official, sparked off *La Guerre des Bouffons*, which the French won, largely because the Italians thought it was a competition to discover who could eat the most.

Opera did not recover from this controversary until a German called Willy the Bald came to Paris and said "Back to 1600," thus becoming the first of many to re-orchestrate Monty Verdi's *Orfeo.*

It is difficult to know why Willy the Bald said this, although, as he said it in German, it is possible to blame the translation.

### The Discovery of the Symphony

This took place in Mannheim, Germany, by various composers called Stamitz, who realized it should be in E$b$ major and the first movement should be in

First Movement Form. This was not as simple as it might appear, since at the time no one knew what First Movement Form was.

One of Stamitz' friends thought it might be the same as Sonata Form, but Stamitz shook his head and said, "That's as maybe and you may be right, but I intend to find out by Trial and Error."

So he wrote *Allegro* at the top of his manuscript paper and then started the piece with a pretty dull tune on the notes of the Eb chord. In fact, it was so dull that he asked his wife if she would be kind enough to write the next one for him.

This she did, and not surprisingly it turned out to be more feminine than the first, although unfortunately she wrote it in Bb major because that was what she thought he'd said.

In spite of this, Stamitz accepted it and filled the bits in between with a lot of arpeggios for the violins to play because he thought they needed the practice. Then he wrote a double bar and a repeat mark so that they got more of it.

"I have now exposed my tunes," he said, "I shall therefore call it the Exposition. Now I must develop them."

Later he realized this thought was crucial to the whole scheme, and what he did next was truly amazing. He put his dull tune in the bass and made the violins do their arpeggio practice on top!

Although he could see this was pretty good, it only lasted for about four bars, so he had a rest for a moment while he waited for another crucial thought to come, which it did: He did the same thing again in another key!

At this point, the whole process began to get a grip on him and he kept doing the same thing in another key until he found himself back in Eb by mistake.

He recognized it immediately.

"This is the Recapitulation," he said, using a word he had found in *Roget's Thesaurus* meaning, "say what you first said all over again."

So that is what he did, on the way correcting his wife's silly mistake by putting her tune properly in E♭.

At which, he sank back in his chair, well pleased.

He had cracked First Movement Form. All he had to do now was to write a slow movement, a Minuet and a Rondo and he had a Symphony on his hands.

This he accomplished without difficulty, and he called it *Symphony No.1 in Eb,* to differentiate it from all the other *Symphonies in Eb* he now proposed to write.

As the Mannheim Orchestra had two oboes and two horns as well as strings, it can be seen how striking was the effect of this new art form.

*Review V*

Say anything you like about *le Douanier* Jean-Jacques Rousseau.

Does the fact that Stamitz' wife mis-heard him mean Stamitz had a speech defect?

What was the name of the Padre in Pergolesi's opera of the same name?

Did Stamitz write any symphonies that were *not* in E♭?

What was Lully doing with his baton when he hit his foot with it?

Write out a Menu for the *Guerre des Bouffons* and suggest a restaurant.

Say "Back to 1600" in German.

## Chapter 6

*The Piano*

The news can be withheld no longer. The piano had at last been invented, and a sigh of relief swept through the musical world.

First Movement Form was immediately renamed Sonata Form so the Piano Sonata could be born, and Harpsichords, despite their long lineage and their undoubted success as kits for home construction, were thrown on the scrap heap.

Teachers of the new instrument began putting up cards in newsagents' windows and Leeds and Moscow made preparations for international competitions.

There was, however, one problem: What was it to be called?

Nowadays it is called the Steinway or, more usually, the Yamaha, but one can see why, in the 18th century, there was some hesitation about calling it the *Zumpe & Buntebart.*

The Fortepiano was suggested because it could play both loudly and softly and the Pianoforte for precisely the opposite reason. It was the English who, with their gift for paradox (see Shakespeare), finally decided on the Piano because they said it was so loud.

The importance of the piano is seminal. You weren't allowed to be a composer or a conductor or even a musicologist without learning it. Nor, for that matter, could you be a pianist.

You could be a violinist or a reduced version of an oboeist or a timpanist, but only just.

In conservatoires all over Europe it became known as *The Second Study* and as such it was universally hated. Conductors were automatically chosen from the ranks of pianists and there was only one thing regarded as more respectable than the piano and that was the organ, because it could be regarded as a sort of orchestra in miniature.

However, as only the very rich could afford an organ in their sitting room, the piano eventually became accepted as the poor man's substitute and anyone who could not play it was looked down upon. For one thing, how could a composer play his works to his publisher if he couldn't play the piano?

On the other hand, by a strange twist of fate, composers who were known to write their music "at the keyboard" were thought to be less accomplished than those wrote away from it.

Playing the piano became, to a musician, the equivalent of being able to spell or add up, and two sorts of pianists soon emerged – those who could "read at sight" and those who were able to play concertos. It was impossible to do both.

### Haydn and Mozart

It has been said that although Stamitz discovered the symphony, it was Haydn who invented it. He did this by realizing it didn't have to be in E♭ and that the first movement needn't have a second tune if your wife wasn't up to it. If she wasn't, the movement would then be called *Monogamous*, which Haydn usually was, except with singers.

Haydn himself came from a family of wheelwrights, and if he had stuck to that trade he would have been all right. Unfortunately he decided to learn to sing and then go to Vienna as a chorister. As a result, his voice broke and he would have been castrated if his father hadn't stepped in and forbade it, although in view of the lady Haydn later married, this might have been no bad thing.

Instead of singing, Haydn learned the violin and then discovered he had a talent for writing music, which was what he decided to do for the rest of his life.

Being a composer in those days was a highly regarded profession – something that even Dukes, Princes and Royalty admired – whereas today it is thought of, if at all, as what people do in between teaching.

However, as Haydn's reputation spread throughout Europe, teaching became what he did in between composing. In fact, he wrote so much it took 40 closely written pages to fit all of it into the catalogue. It was said Haydn couldn't see a page of blank manuscript paper without wanting to fill it with notes, in which case it was surprising they were all so good.

If Haydn invented the symphony, Mozart invented practically everything else including the piano concerto, the string quartet and billiards. In spite of his brilliance, he was a modest man, preferring to write under the assumed name of Kochel and refer to his pieces by numbers. Hence, "did you hear *K.272* last night?" and similar remarks.

Some people say Mozart invented opera as well, but this is nonsense because he was too late. He did, however, invent Mozart Opera, in which people sung about different things at the same time whilst trying to remember where they came in next.

Unlike Haydn, Mozart grew up in a musical family and was so precocious that his father, Leopold, took him on a tour of Europe when he was eight to show him off.

Thus, while Haydn worked most of his life as a servant in the household of Prince Esterhazy, Mozart flitted from place to place like a butterfly and thus died nearly 20 years earlier than Haydn.

Because of this, his catalogue runs only to 20 pages as opposed to Haydn's 40, which means their average output per year was about the same. It is not generally known that Mozart was christened Johannes Chrisostomus Wolfgangus Theophilus.

## The Viennese Tradition

With the advent of Haydn and Mozart, the Viennese realized it was time they made a bid for Austria to be Top Musical Nation and they did this by making everyone a Professor and then building lots of coffeehouses where they could talk, write or read newspapers on sticks.

They also invented the Vienna Philharmonic Orchestra and made it play not quite together (Wiener Schlamperei) and founded the Austro-Hungarian Empire so they could get in some decent Czech violinists and call them Austrians. They also invented the waltz and lots of people called Strauss to write them, calling the whole edifice The First Viennese School so they could have a Second later on.

Various other things contributed to this great tradition, including the Vienna Boys Choir, Sachertorte and the Riding School Horses' Opera Ball.

There was also a ball for people called The Vienna Opera Ball, which took place in the State Opera House and which was so expensive that no one could afford to go to it except players in the Vienna Philharmonic Orchestra, who were paid to do so.

Vienna was also important for the Heuriger, an annual (or sometimes Bi-or-Triannual) drink-up in Grinzing, a suburb of Vienna where members of the Vienna Philharmonic went to earn an honest schilling playing waltzes in gardens.

Because Beethoven had once lived in Grinzing, it also became fashionable to look for his house with a glass in one hand and a bottle in the other. As there was scarcely a corner of Vienna in which Beethoven had not lived at one time or another, this eventually became a well-known game called *Bezirking* and was played by English tourists after Philharmonic concerts.

All in all, it was agreed that the Austrians were as good at music as the Germans but had bigger vibratos.

*Review VI*

Who do you suspect of being Zumpe
& Buntebart?

With which singer was Haydn not
monogamous?

Write a very short essay and put it on a
stick.

Is it Wiener Schlamperei if the Boston
Symphony don't play together?

Do you know how to play a Heuriger?

Describe The Riding School Horses
Opera Ball.

Is a Heuriger a dance in 6/8 time or a brand
of champagne?

*Revision VI* continued

Do you know a Concert Pianist who can also read at sight? If so, please inform the Editor.

Where would you go to earn an honest pfund?

Describe why Beethoven lived in Vienna.

Have you ever written anything in Eb?

# – Chapter 7 –

*Beethoven*

As soon as Napoleon heard that Beethoven was writing a symphony for him, he immediately declared himself Emperor.

Other world figures who owe much to Beethoven include the Duke of Wellington, for whom Beethoven achieved victory at Waterloo by including *God Save the King* in his *Battle Symphony*, and Sir Winston Churchill, to whom Beethoven dedicated the first two bars of his *Fifth Symphony*.

Although he also dedicated works to the sovereigns of Austria, Prussia and Russia, as well as to the Arch-Duke Rudolph, the Princes Lobkowitz, Galitsin, von Lichnowsky, Radziwill, von Schwarzenberg and the Counts Rasumovsky, von Fries, Oppersdorf, von Browne and their wives, Beethoven was a rugged Republican at heart.

Of his nine symphonies, the odd numbers were the greatest, although numbers *II, IV, VI* and *VIII* were only slightly less good because everything Beethoven wrote was good except his *Triple Concerto*.

Beethoven also reinvented the Development Section. He had studied these with Haydn and did some notable things with them that were a far cry from Stamitz and his arpeggios, which Beethoven used to refer to scathingly as "Stamitz and his archipeligos."

Something else Beethoven learnt from Haydn was the "false entry" – viz. his horn-call two bars early in the *Eroica Symphony* – and if someone failed to comment on these, Beethoven would fly into a fury and say things like, "You're the result of a false entry yourself, *dumkopf!*" He had a mercurial sense of humor that did not always endear him to everyone, particularly if he pulled the chair away from someone just about to sit down – a joke of which he was especially proud, and which used to send him into paroxysms of laughter.

However, he was a good friend to people he liked, such as Maelzel, whose invention (the metronome) he made use of to indicate the speed of his movements.

Because some of these MMs, as they were called, sounded too fast, it became fashionable to maintain that Beethoven's metronome must have been faulty and some meticulous critics have even gone so far as to buy an 18th-century metronome and some 18th-century oil to put in it, in order to prove their point.

So far, the only point they've proved is that a Metronome is *not* a little man running round the Paris underground, which is what most people knew anyway.

Another reason why Beethoven's metronome must have been right was that he had the results printed in the *Wiener Zeitung*, which was a newspaper of such immense seriousness that there was no question of anyone doubting it. Another notable result of this controversy controversy was that some conductors spent the rest of their lives trying to beat faster.

Although program music had not yet been invented, Beethoven was so much in advance of his time that he wrote some of it in his *Sixth Symphony* (The Pastoral). The first movement he called "Awakening with cheerful feelings on the arrival of the country" and it was such a success that he promptly wrote four more, all of them with funny titles, of which the second was about a man sitting next door to Bach.

Toward the end of his life, Beethoven began going deaf and people were quick to point out that this must be why his music was beginning to sound so peculiar, which it was. Few could understand why it kept changing its mood for no apparent reason until Beethoven wrote a letter called *The Heiligenstadt Testament,* in which he describes how difficult it is to write good music anyway, and particularly if you are going deaf.

After that, people began to accept the abrupt changes of mood in his music and believe that perhaps Beethoven was not going peculiar after all. Some even said that perhaps he was as great as Shakespeare or Goethe, and that he was certainly greater than Stamitz.

This last thought pleased Beethoven considerably, and put him in such a good humor that he decided to write a *Choral Symphony* in which the four solo singers would have to sit still for the first three movements and then get up and sing a quartet of such appalling difficulty that Beethoven only just managed not to laugh out loud every time they tried to sing it. He used to refer to it as his *Ode to Joy* because it gave him so much innocent pleasure.

It was used by the English Labour Party as their party song for an election not so long ago – the one they lost.

*Schubert and the Lied*

Schubert's great achievement was to invent the *Lied*, and with it, Lieder Recitals, Lieder competitions and master classes.

Unfortunately, he insisted his *Lied* must always be sung in German so no one could understand them unless they bought a program, and then only just.

Two of his most famous cycles were to words by the poet Wilhelm Muller – *Winterreise* (A Winter Holiday) and *Die Schone Mullerin* (The Beautiful Mrs. Muller).

Schubert also wrote eight or nine symphonies of which the *Seventh* or *Ninth* was nearly as long as Beethoven's *Ninth,* and sometimes longer. His most popular symphony was his shortest – the *Eighth* – often called *The Unfinished* because Schubert left the last two movements behind in one of the coffeehouses he was wont to frequent.

Schubert was often to be found in these, seated in a corner seat, smoking a clay pipe and sipping *Gluwein* whilst he nodded affectionately to his friends as they passed by. When they didn't pass by, they would sit down next to him and buy him some more *Gluwein,* which explains what happened to his *Eighth Symphony.*

Apart from his symphonies and songs, Schubert also wrote chamber music, including the *String Quintet in C*, the slow movement of which has been played more times on Desert Island Discs than any other work.

Schubert was born and died in Vienna and was thus known as an "Echt-Wiener," which was what Napoleon used to call his Frankfurters-on-rye when he was living there. In those days, Vienna was a small town, bounded by the Danube Canal on one side and enclosed by ramparts on the others, and that was the way Schubert liked it. He didn't want to have to walk too far from one coffeehouse to the next looking for the remainder of his symphony, nor did he want too many things such as *Gluweins* or ladies distracting him from his composition.

As he was fond of saying, he had only about another six years to live and he needed those for the remaining 150 works he intended writing. He was right on both counts.

*Brahms*

Brahms was nearly as great as Beethoven but not quite. People realized this when he tried to write Beethoven's *Ode to Joy* theme for the finale of his *First Symphony*, but got it wrong.

He spent his early years in Hamburg, sitting on the knees of prostitutes while he played the piano, and it has been suggested that this is why he never married. However, he was a good friend of Robert Schumann's wife, Clara, for many years.

Brahms greatly enjoyed putting one tune in the treble and another in the bass and then changing them around, and for relaxation he would drink strong black coffee and smoke cigars. His tastes were simple apart from the fact that he decided to spend the last 35 years of his life in Vienna.

He wrote four symphonies, of which numbers *1, 2,* and *4* are the most popular. The *Third* is less so because it has a quiet ending and is not easy to conduct.

When an orchestral manager says: "We'd better have some Brahms this year," the music director usually says: "Then we'll do the *First* – we haven't done that for ages."

He forgets that they've done it every year since he arrived because it's his favourite. This is because it has a "sturm und drang" beginning and because there is a horn solo in the finale that is sometimes played on the flute. It also contains Brahms' best tune (see para.1).

Brahms' early career as a pub pianist in the brothels of Hamburg received a welcome interruption when Reményi a Hungarian violinist, asked him to be his accompanist for a tour of Europe, although what Remenyi was doing in Brahms' brothel remains a mystery to this day.

However, the invitation led to Brahms being introduced to Joachim (violinist), Liszt (pianist) and Robert Schumann (composer), all of whom helped him become known to a wider audience.

Brahms was a quiet, modest man, but he got on with people.

It was about this time that Liszt and Wagner jointly headed The Neo-German Party, the aims of which were unclear save that they supported the ideals behind the music each of them wrote. The ideal was Romanticism.

Brahms and Joachim would have none of this. They thought music should be about music, not about stories, and so everyone should know how they felt, they wrote a protest in the *Neue Zeitschrift fur Musik* – an otherwise respectable magazine – saying how wrong they thought Liszt and Wagner were.

It was an inflamatory piece that asked all true artists and music-lovers to join their ranks. They demanded action, and their hope was that all old Germans like themselves would write to the *Neue Zeitschrift* supporting their aims. Two of them did.

Liszt and Wagner were very decent about the whole episode and pretended they didn't mind, although when Hanslick (a critic who was a very Old German) began writing nasty articles about them, they thought that perhaps they did mind after all.

At first, no one was very clear about the differences between the two sides, but in the end it was generally accepted that Liszt and Wagner liked stories and Brahms and Joachim didn't.

The only real winner was Hanslick, because it gave him something to write about in his newspaper and ensured that his name would be remembered by posterity. Just as we've done here.

### Schumann, Mendelssohn and Chopin

These composers have so little in common with each other it is hard to see why they are grouped together.

Could it be that Schumann thought Mendelssohn's music facile and worthless or that Mendelssohn thought Schumann's inept and clumsy, or both?

If so, what was Chopin's opinion? Did it worry him that Mendelssohn was a Jew or was it his habit of naming his symphonies that Chopin found objectionable?

Finally, is there any evidence that the three of them ever met?

If they did, could it have been in Rostock, where Clara Schumann gave some concerts in 1843?

Did Schumann propose that he accompany her, and if so would this have persuaded Mendelssohn to make the arduous journey himself? If it did, would he have asked Chopin to join him?

This seems doubtful, although it may be significant that both Schumann and Chopin were born in 1810 and Mendelssohn in 1809.

Did it occur to them that Chopin's death in 1849 coincided with the socialist uprising in Dresden, from which both Schumann and his wife fled in terror, or was this was mere coincidence?

If so, there is a further complication that bears examination: It is known that Chopin based his *Nocturnes* on those of the Irish composer John Field, who died in 1837 in Moscow, and further that Schumann was much given to using secret letter-codes in his piano music.

However, neither Schumann nor Mendelssohn ever visited Moscow(!) Nor, for that matter did Chopin, although he was born in Zelazowa Wola, Poland.

Why not?

It is possible that these, and other questions will never be answered. For example, shall we ever know why Chopin had a long affair with a man called George Sands and yet received a thousand pounds from a Scottish lady aptly named Miss Stirling?

Is it true that the cross-rhythms in the finale of Schumann's *Piano Concerto* were also a code, and if so were they ever sent to John Field in Moscow?

If they were, they were eight years too late, but would Schumann have known this? If not, so be it. More interesting, perhaps, is whether John Field ever got the cross-rhythms right. If he did, he would have realized they were a palindrome based on his own *Third Nocturne.* (N.B.: It should not be forgotten that in 1849 Schumann wrote an unpublished piece in two movements for *Harmonium*!)

*Review VII*

Was Beethoven responsible for the retreat from Moscow?

Write 1,000 words on *The Beautiful Mrs Muller*, and say why.

Have you ever been to Zelazowa Wola, and do you intend going?

Write a cross-rhythm and send it to Moscow.

Did you ever meet George Sands and was he homosexual?

Say what you like about Brahms' early years.

# – Chapter 8 –

## The Romantic Movement

"Oh, mighty Weber," said Berlioz, in French.

Although Weber was the cousin of Mozart's wife, he was also a daring innovator. He founded the Romantic Movement by writing operas in German, and on receiving a commission from Covent Garden to write one in English, he wrote *Oberon* and died.

So successful was Weber at being German that both Liszt and Wagner immediately called themselves Neo-Germans to show they were on his side, and then went on to consolidate the Romantic Movement by inventing the Symphonic Poem and the Music Drama, respectively.

In the Symphonic Poem, Liszt attempted something that had never been tried before – namely, to tell a story without using singers. First, he would choose a subject in which everyone was interested, such as *Hunnenschlacht* or *Die Ideale* or *Von der Wiege bis zum Grabe*, and then he would write a tune. This tune he would change according to what happened, but it would always be the same tune!

He called this invention the Transformation of Themes, and it became so popular that everyone started using it, especially Wagner, who called it a Light Motive and used one per Light, Ring, Sword, River, God, Swan etc. in his Music Dramas.

Berlioz also tried to be a Neo-German, but failed because he was French and couldn't play the piano. Nevertheless he adopted Liszt's ideas when he became obsessed with an English actress he had never met called Harriet Smithson, whom he called his *Idee Fixe*, and whom he kept putting in all sorts of impossible situations, such as riding with a coven of witches on a broomstick or listening to a concert of his works.

All this he portrayed in a piece called *Symphonie Fantastique* or *Episodes in the Life of an Artist,* in which he also produced a thunderstorm that went on for a quarter-of-an-hour without stopping. This had not been done before, although Beethoven had tried and failed.

When it became clear that Berlioz could portray, by purely orchestral means, a head rolling off the executioner's block or any Fixed Idea you cared to mention, the French government decided to give him the *Prix de Rome,* which entitled him to a year's scholarship in Rome, during which time he could write music and absorb Rome's classical past.

To celebrate this – as he had still not met Miss Smithson – Berlioz decided to fall in love with a pianist called Camille Moke, who promptly jilted him and married a M. Pleyel, who made the pianos that Berlioz could not play.

Berlioz was not happy in Rome, partly because he met Mendelssohn, whom he didn't like, and partly because of Ms. Moke, so he decided to eschew Rome's classical past and return to Paris.

There, he at once began organizing an Autobiographical Concert, at which the guest of honor would be Miss Harriet Smithson, whom he had still not met.

Berlioz also wrote a sequel to his *Symphonie Fantastique* for the occasion, called *Lelio* or *Return To Life,* which showed, in appalling detail, how much the Artist (Berlioz) had suffered for his Fixed Ideas.

So horrified was Miss Smithson at this portrayal of a man she had never even seen that she at once said, "Show me to him," and then married him to make up for it.

Meanwhile, Berlioz was busy writing another work about himself in which he took the part of a solo viola. It was called *Harold in Italy* and it was so loosely based on Lord Byron that no one noticed. It took place in the mountains of Abruzzi and the first section portrayed Harold's melancholy, then his happiness and finally his joy. There followed a movement about pilgrims chanting as they made their way through the mountains whilst having an affair with a mountaineer's mistress and it finished with a group of brigands having an orgy.

Paganini was to have played the viola part, but once he saw that it had no fingered octaves he said he wouldn't, so Berlioz composed a *Funereal and Triumphant Symphony* with no violas that was to be performed by military bands marching through the streets of Paris in the rain.

He also wrote an opera on the subject of Benvenuto Cellini, who made salt-cellars. For the carnival scene at which everyone shook salt-cellars at each other, Berlioz wrote *Le Carnival Romain,* which later became popular as an overture in its own right, the part of the salt-cellars being taken by tambourines.

Berlioz' second opera was *The Trojans,* and as it was five hours long, he cut it into two halves. Finally, he wrote *Beatrice and Benedick,* based on *Much Ado About Nothing,* which he said was about his wife, Miss Smithson.

According to the writer Theophile Gautier, Berlioz represented the perfect type of Romantic artist, forming a trinity with Delacroix and Victor Hugo. Berlioz was also well known as a critic, which meant he was able to say mean things about other people's music without having to apologize later.

*Wagner and the Music Drama*

Wagner's longest Music Drama concerned the adventures of a Ring from the moment it was stolen from the River Maidens to another moment, four days later, when they got it back.

His other Music Dramas included *Tristan and Isolde* (about profane and sacred love) *Parsifal* (about Free-masonry) and *The Mastersingers* (about singing competitions).

If a Grand Opera is a series of arias and ensembles occasionally interrupted by a plot, Music Drama is a series of plots occasionally interrupted by arias and ensembles. It refuses to wait while the composer describes how his characters are feeling but puts it all in the orchestra instead.

Music Drama has several unusual features that bear discussion. For instance, if Wotan (the God) is talking to Brunnhilde, Wagner will give them both their own tune so that he can play them together if they fit. If they don't, he won't, but he usually made sure they did.

If Brunnhilde was miserable (which she often was), Wagner would write her tune in a miserable version and Wotan's in a happy one (if he was happy). This ensures that the audience know how the characters feel without holding things up.

The intertwining of Brunnhilde's and Wotan's tunes was not Wagner's only resource. He also had a large orchestra in the pit against which the singers would try to be heard, and very often the orchestra would tell you more about the plot than the protaganists.

Thus, if Siegfried is on the stage but the orchestra begins playing the Rhine Maiden's theme, you can be sure Siegfried is thinking about them, unless Wagner got the plot wrong, which he rarely did.

Should you hear Valkyries singing "Hoy-hoy" off stage, watch out for them to arrive, flying on ropes. If you hear a lot of harps and rushing strings, you can bet that Valhalla is burning somewhere nearby.

If the whole cast is standing, not moving, and dressed in long dressing-gowns, you have got the date wrong and are listening to *Parsifal* instead.

So the audience could feel there was nothing coming between them and the action, Wagner asked King Ludwig to build him a special opera house in which the orchestra pit was underneath the stage. This simple device also allowed the audience to occasionally hear what was being sung on stage.

Wagner was not only a great innovator, he was also a talented writer whose books achieved great popularity in Germany in the 1930s. In real life, he liked to dress up in silk dressing-gowns and marry chorus girls if possible.

*The Development of the Orchestra*

What would one of Wagner's Music Dramas have sounded like on an orchestra of two oboes, two horns and strings?

Not so good, must be the answer.

The reason orchestras developed (i.e. got bigger) are either socio-political or politico-social, depending on what you call the rise of the middle classes.

Not many princes, dukes etc. were able to house an orchestra big enough to perform a Liszt tone poem, nor could they afford enough musicians on salary with full pension rights to play it.

Thus the concert hall was invented, and with it the freelance, self-employed musician (see Schedule D). New instruments were needed to express the new ideas composers were beginning to have, and vice versa.

For instance:

*Bass-clarinet Ideas*: brooding love, or water gurgling down a plug-hole.

*Double-bassoon Ideas*: nameless things crawling out of swamps.

*Cor anglais Ideas*: plangent thoughts about Nature, Trees, Bushes, Snakes, etc.

*Harp Ideas*: spiritual matters or Greek vases.

*Three Trombone Ideas*: noble thoughts or (if muted) exactly the opposite.

*Piccolo Ideas*: Reinforcing the high bits the first violins can't play.

*Eb Clarinet Ideas*: Witches on broomsticks or making the whole woodwind section sound out-of-tune.

*Timpani Ideas*: Thunder storms or *God Save the Queen.*

*Tubular Bell Ideas*: *1812* Ideas.

*Side drum Ideas*: Ideas about Ravel's *Bolero.*

*Organ Ideas*: Great Gate of Kiev Ideas.

Altogether, it is not surprising that, between 1780 and 1890, the orchestra grew from 0200.2000.T. Strgs, to 4444.4331.T & P.Hp.Strgs. Is it?

In order to accomodate such large numbers, platforms had to get bigger and an elaborate system of semaphore developed so the conductor's intentions could reach the back of the orchestra. It is not surprising to know that Berlioz was once more in the forefront of these new developements, adding to his large work on orchestration a *Handbook of Conducting* in which he insisted that all orchestras should have 32 harps.

## The Development of the Conductor

Once Orchestras had become 4444. etc, the need for someone to tell them which bits to practise become apparent. This function the Conductor performs.

The founder of the modern school of conducting was Richard Wagner, as can be seen by referring to the *London Times* (1860): "The season during which Wagner conducted the Philharmonic Orchestra was one of the most disastrous on record."

As a result, many conductors do not stay in one place very long.

There are two sorts of conductor – the Guest Conductor and the Music Director – and they have been referred to respectively as having a brief affair as opposed to getting married.

The guest conductor does not need the wide repertoire of the music director because he can usually tour the same program around the world several times before he gets found out.

It has been said of the music director that he discovers the strengths and weaknesses of his orchestra only too well and vice versa.

A good music director is fortunate in being able to form a close relationship between himself and his orchestra, whereas all the guest conductor can do is to take the next train home.

# 1812 And all That

## The Great Composer-Pianists

The most important factor in discussing these remarkable musicians is to distinguish between Composer-Pianists and Pianist-Composers. A system for achieving this has already been worked out by the Performing Rights Society, using a simple first-past-the-post points system:

1. To be a Composer-Pianist, it is necessary to have written five minutes of music for every public recital given.

2. To be a Pianist-Composer, one must have given at least two hundred recitals in *bona fide* halls. (Villages with a population of less than 25 not eligible.)

3. An application form, giving all performance details, should be filled in, together with the nature of the compositions being offered: i.e: Sonatas, Lyric pieces or Tone poems, Symphonies, Operas or Ballets.

4. In the case of orchestral works, the number of pages of full score will be aggregated and then divided by the number of public appearances as follows: X x 200 = 200 X or (a+b = *+*). Thus, 250 X = b+c, 4/6 + ***

Assuming the orchestration falls below 4444.4431.-T&P.Hp, then deduct b+c,4/6+*** & move 205 to the power of a=b=***. Correct reply: 24 per minute.

On the basis of this system, Liszt was voted top of the Composer-Pianists with Rachmaninoff coming a close second.

Busoni became winner of the Pianist-Composer category, followed by Schnabel, for whom, because of the density of his only symphony, a special category had to be introduced at his own request.

An interesting case was Prokofiev because it emerged that a third party had been engaged for the orchestration of *Romeo and Juliet*, also because *Peter and the Wolf* didn't fit easily into any of the above-mentioned categories.

It was later agreed that none of these categories existed before 1840 (thus automatically ruling out Mozart), and that any attempts to propose new members into the society should be automatically refused until referred to the Arts Council Appeals Tribunal, which usually meant the same thing. A good example of the appeals procedure was Saint-Saëns, a strong contender from the start, although his *Carnival of the Animals* threw some doubt over the decision, but when questions were asked in the French National Assembly as to whether he should be subjected to this sort of scrutiny, the Second World War had been declared and all lists were prematurely closed, never to be reopened.

*The Eccentrics*

This has never been a proper group with its own agenda and constitution, or even with a named membership. Rather, various musicians have been put forward from time to time, from Gesualdo to Paganini, although whether murdering one's own child by violently rocking its cradle (Gesualdo) was eccentricity before it was murder or the other way round has always been open to debate.

Nor has it been assumed that the hallucinations of Schumann and Hugo Wolf came under this heading. Rather, the fact that they both ended their days in asylums indicated genuine illness rather than mental abberations, even if the hallucinations themselves might well have qualified.

A more convincing candidate has always been Eric Satie, for running round his audience shouting "Parlez! Parlez!" because they had stopped talking and were actually listening to his *Musique d'Ameublement*.

Hector Berlioz qualified on two counts: Neither his life nor his music was normal. He decided to make his reputation as an eccentric and it spilt over into his creative life.

The same thing happened in the 1930s to a pianist called Vladimir Pachmann. In the middle of one of his London recitals, he leant down toward the audience and said: "Listen to this ... is it not beautiful? ... so tender?" His audience was enraptured to find the soloist confiding in this way, especially as he did it every time there was a flowing tune.

After a bit, they noticed he never leant forward during the difficult bits, but it was enough that he was so moved by the easy bits that he felt impelled to talk to them about it.

And so to Paganini – something of a Faustian figure who sold his soul to the Devil in exchange for an amazing technique. This did not, however, rob him of his native cunning – was there ever another soloist who used to sell his tickets from the box office and then return to the Green Room to change and start the concert?

Perhaps he sold his soul on condition that the Devil broke all his strings one by one starting with the top E string, so Paganini was forced to play everything extremely high up on the lower strings.

Kaikhosru Sorabji was an eccentric in precisely the opposite way. He was a composer-pianist who wrote terrifyingly difficult piano music and then refused to allow anyone to play it.

When this unusual trait got around, a gasp of relief swept through the musical world. Few fates, after all, could have been more dreadful than learning one of those pieces only to be taken to court the next day and sued.

It may be that Sorabji was the way he was because he was born in Chingford. Perhaps he had eccentricity thrust upon him.

*Review VIII*

Say "O, mighty Weber" in French.

Translate *"Von der Wiege bis zum Grabe"* into English and back again.

Which is your favorite day in Wagner's *Ring?*

Explain 4444.4331.T&P.Hp.Strgs. so that it makes sense.

Who wrote the *Times* review of Wagner's concerts and what happened to him afterwards?

Think of an Idea for an Alto-flute.

Describe the Rise of the Middle Classes.

Did Wagner write a Music Drama about King Ludwig? Why not?

Who was the French Wagner?

Have you ever discussed Paganini with a well-known eccentric?

# – Chapter 9 –

## What is Opera?

### Grand Opera

Grand Opera means Opera where the orchestra play all the time but you listen to the singers – as opposed to Music Drama, where the singers sing all the time but you listen to the orchestra.

It should not be confused with *Opera Buffa*, *Opera Comique*, *Singspiel* or Gilbert and Sullivan, which are performed in smaller theatres with lower ticket prices.

In order to justify the higher prices and white ties, composers of Grand Opera began looking for libretti with ever more exotic subject matter. Meyerbeer led the field with *Emma di Leicester*, followed by Donizetti's *Emilia di Liverpool* and Auber's closely plotted *Le Chateau de Kenilworth*.

Bizet, finding towns being used up at a phenomenal rate, had to make do with Perth, while the young Welsh composer Goring Thomas, who had been going to write an opera about Swansea, changed his mind and called it *The Light of the Harem*.

In the end, it was Verdi who came out on top with *Aida*, which had a Chorus of Camels and was written for the Grand Opening of the Sewage Canal at Luxor.

Other subjects that have been found suitable for Grand Opera are characters from Russian history, especially Boris Godunov and Prince Igor. It is interesting that no one has yet written a Grand Opera on the life of Napoleon, Lenin, George Washington, Peter Abelard or Rasputin. The author has a few libretti of his own on these subjects and would be happy to post them to any interested party for an initial subscription of £25 ($37 USD/ $55 CND) plus self-addressed envelope, with postage.

*Opera Comique*

This means *The Tales of Hoffmann* in France, *Die Fledermaus* in Austria and Gilbert and Sullivan in England. All these operettas use spoken dialogue and their place has now been taken by Musicals.

The lineage, however, is clear. The place of the old Fourth-act Ballets has been taken by the Dream Sequence, a set of dances meant to summarize the plot so far. And funny monologues such as the Jailor's in *Fledermaus* have been replaced by "in-front-of-tabs" comics. Plus ça change ...

Because opera afficionados do not find operettas serious enough, and since the people who used to go to them now go to musicals instead, the genre has suffered a sharp decline, although the old favorites are regularly brought out and dusted down by amateur companies in Guildford, Oban and Barnsley.

By now it must be clear that opera has always been divided between the French, the Germans and the Italians, and that the Germans have usually won because of being Top Musical Nation.

In spite of this, a enthusiastic minority have always maintained that Italian opera is best because Italian vowel sounds made people sing better and because Puccini had all the best plots.

French opera was generally considered too light and frothy to be taken seriously in spite of *Pelleas and Melisande*, which was rarely performed because Melisande insisted on throwing her hair over the balcony for Pelleas to climb up. This was considered too dangerous a coup to do more than once a season.

Nor was much notice taken of operas from other European countries, such as *Dalibor,* which no one went to hear because it was written in Czech. On the other hand, those same people *did* go to the other Czech opera,

*The Bartered Bride*, largely because the title was written in German (*Die Ver- kaufte Braut*) and therefore the piece was thought to be OK. If it had remained in the repertoire as *Prtodnaya Vesti*, its success might well have been more doubtful.

There was also, of course, the problem of whether Russian opera should be taken seriously or not.

Everyone knew that Russian ballet should, because of Tchaikovsky and Petipa and the fact that all Russian dancers could jump higher than anyone else, but Russian opera was another matter.

First of all, it was about a series of Russian Csars no one had ever heard of and then it was sung by some very large Russian basses who could all reach bottom C if they took enough breaths.

Furthermore, they were nearly all set in St. Basil's Cathedral, which consisted of hundreds of small rooms, through which the Czar could creep, listening to other people's conversations.

In fact, Russian Opera really came to life only when the Russian people began singing about what dreadful lives they had and how it would only get better when the Czar had been deposed and replaced by another.

Naturally, Russian opera shared with Czech opera the disadvantage that no one could understand what anyone was saying and this raised the whole question of the relationship between opera and language.

Is it better to know what's going on or not?

Sometimes, of course, not.

There can be few operagoers who have not been totally absorbed in the music and the emotional situation only to realize later that the man was only trying to sell his coat.

More recently, of course, there have been subtitles for opera just as there were sub-titles for films, and these have been a good thing because they not only allow you to understand the plot, but they also enable you to see how Alf and Bert were getting on letting down the backdrops from the flies.

Other ways of understanding foreign operas are to get there an hour early and try to understand what is going to happen from the almost incomprehensible program notes, or to refuse to go to them unless they have been translated into English.

It should be understood that the latter course is no guarantee one will be able to understand what is being said because of the great difference between spoken and sung English. Sung English has no consonants and only one vowel sound.

Is this important?

Time and motion experts have worked out that, by the time you have listened to the music, worked out which character is which, examined the sets, watched the conductor and waited for an available toilet, there is no time to do anything else anyway.

They maintain that the best way to listen to opera is to shut your eyes and allow your imagination to do the rest.

After all, does it really matter if you listen to the sextet from *Figaro* thinking everyone is discussing who is going to stay to dinner?

There is one sort of opera, of course, in which the words are always heard. This is called Gilbert and

Sullivan, and it occurs because the management are so insistent that none of Gilbert's words be lost that they fire anyone who allows it.

To which, there is only one further question – is Gilbert and Sullivan really opera? There is no easy answer to this, so it will not be addressed later.

### The French Organ School

This was invented by two composers who decided the Romantic Movement was getting out of hand but would be all right if it were played on the organ. They were laughingly known as Cesar Franc and Vingt-cent D'Indy because they wanted to start a fee-paying private music school in Paris to prove that French music could be as serious as German if played slowly enough.

Eventually, Vingt-cent had to start this project on his own because Cesar Franc got run over by a tram.

However, Vingt-Cent made a very good start by calling it the *Schola Cantorum* and later it became extremely successful, sending organists all over the world to play the organ symphonies of King Vidor.

The reason for the *Schola Cantorum*'s success was that it tapped into a deep schism in the French character. Although it was evident to everyone that the French could write *morceaux de salon* better than anyone else, this was exactly what the French didn't want. They wanted profundity, and that was what the *Schola Cantorum* offered them.

First of all, the name was in Latin and then there was the conviction, undisputed anywhere in France, that French organs and French organists were the best in the world.

Finally, it was made clear by the *Schola Cantorum* that all their organ soloists must leave a piece of music in their hotel room by mistake so they can ask the audience for a theme on which they can improvise later.

*Review IX*

Comment briefly on Emma di Leicester and add a short character analysis.

For "Sewage" read "Suez" and give a reason for this ridiculous mistake.

What was the number of the tram that ran over Cesar Franc?

What does "idiosyncracy" really mean?

Who was the French Reger?

When was Saint-Saëns beatified?

Write an opera on Napoleon using the editor's libretto.

Leave a piece of music in your hotel room and improvise on it.

Imagine an opera and then write a précis.

Would you like to see Alf and Bert's flies if you had the chance?

# – Chapter 10 –

## The Rise of Nationalism

This was yet another attempt by various minorities to prove they were as good as the Germans.

### The Bohemians

These were Smetana and Dvorak, and although Smetana wrote tone poems like Liszt and Dvorak wrote symphonies like Brahms, they were both capable of writing operas if they had to.

However, although everyone knew that Smetana wrote *The Bartered Bride*, there are still many quite well-informed people who are not sure which of them wrote *Branibori v Cechach, Tvrde Palice* or *Kral a Uhlif.*

While Dvorak was in America getting into trouble with the Race Relations Board for writing the ............ Quartet, his publishers muddled up the numbers of his symphonies so no one knew whether *The New World Symphony* was number *V* or *IX*, or if the *D-minor Symphony* was *II, IV* or *VII.*

The three most frequently played of Dvorak's symphonies, therefore, are either *II, IV* and *VIII* or *V, VIII* and *IX* according to which system you favor.

Although Smetana was the senior figure and was thus known as The Father of Czech Music, Dvorak was never known as The Son because it was discovered that he was not as good at opera as Smetana. This was because of his opera *Russalka,* which was about a woman living at the bottom of the Danube who got confused with the other women who lived at the bottom of the Rhine (see Wagner).

In spite of their nationality, both Smetana and Dvorak led well-ordered family lives.

*The Russians*

The Russian Nationalist School began with Glinka and Dargomyszski and it is not difficult to see why Glinka won. Although Glinka worked for the Ministry of Ways and Communications and Dargothingumebob for the Control Department, they both decided to write operas instead. Of these, only one piece is left in the repertoire – the overture to Glinka's *Russlan and Ludmilla*, which lasts for four minutes and thus can be used to boil an egg.

Glinka and his friend were followed by the *The Five*, so called for obvious reasons. The outstanding characteristic of this group was that they rarely finished their pieces themselves, preferring to go around finishing each other's.

Rimsky-Korsakov, particularly, was prone to this habit and it was only with difficulty that he was persuaded not to give a new ending to Borodin's first published work, *On the Action of Ethyl Iodide on Hydrobenzamide and Amarine*. (Borodin was, by profession, a chemist.)

There is little doubt, however, that Mussorgsky and Rimsky were the most talented members of the group, for together they wrote *Boris Godunov, Night on A bald mountain* and *Scheherazade*, but not *Pictures at an Exhibition*, for which venture Moussorgsky teamed up with the well-known French composer Ravel.

Tchaikovsky was never a member of *The Five* because he wasn't nationalist enough. Liadov wasn't because the others had used up all the places and Glinka and his friend were too old.

That left Balakirev, Borodin and Cui (probably pronounced Kwee) who were, and there was little doubt that joining a group with your friends was a good career move.

For example: "Balakirev has just finished a major work for solo piano called *Islamey*. We are reminded that the last piece we heard from this Group was the *Second Symphony* of Borodin, favourably reviewed in this paper, and there seems little doubt that *The Five* are a major force in the musical life of our country. We look forward to Moussorgsky's unfinished opera *Boris Godunov*".

Might Liadov have benefited from this sort of group publicity? Yes, he might.

### Spain

As is well known, all Spanish music was written by Chabrier, Bizet, Ravel and Debussy, often working under their pseudonyms Albeniz, Turina, Granadas and Falla.

However, recent research has uncovered a large amount of real Spanish music in the *Cantinelas Vulgares*, including *Romanceros*, *Villancicos* and *Cantigas* (sometimes with vihuela tablature) whilst in Andalucia one can still hear the *Cante Hondos*, *Cante Flamencos* and *Zapateados* sung and danced to the accompaniment of Gaita, Fluviel or Tenore. Zarzuelas and Sardanas are still being produced in town squares.

There was a real Spanish composer once called Arriaga, but he died at the age of 19.

Also of interest are those Hispano-Spanish composers who settled in South America following the Spanish Conquests. They were accustomed to meet at the notorious Villa Lobos, there to formulate new attitudes towards the music of the Maya, the Incas and the Aztecs.

They formulated one or two quite useful ones, but failed to unearth any written examples, so the Villa Lobos Group, as they were later called, began writing some themselves.

Like Vaughan Williams and Holst, they would travel far into the interior to hear the tribal songs they knew must exist and which they transcribed as they were sung.

The composers who did their best in this way were Lobos himself and Edgar Varese, who wrote a short piece for eight instruments that sounded so like Stravinsky's *Rite of Spring* that he called it *Octandre,* to show that he could manage on eight instruments what Stravinsky accomplished with 120.

Lobos was so obsessed with small trains and J.S. Bach that he wrote several pieces inspired by both. The Lobos group were also friendly with Rivera the painter, and Leon Trotsky the revolutionary (who once sought sanctuary in their villa while he was having an affair with Rivera's wife).

## Hungary

The so-called Gypsy music of Hungary was really Hungarian music played by Gypsies, as opposed to real Gypsy music, which was Gypsy music played by Hungarians. However, Hungarian music, which was composed and played by Hungarians, sounded so similar to Gypsy music, which was composed by Gypsies and played by anyone available, that it was known as Hungarian Peasant music and was thus neither Hungarian nor Gypsy – a fact little understood by Liszt when he wrote *The Gypsies and their music in Hungary* (1859) nor by Kodaly in his *A magyar nepdal strofaszerkezete* (1906).

There is, nevertheless, one real difference between Hungarian and Gypsy music – all Hungarian music is either in 10/8 or 11/16, whereas Gypsy music is all in 4/4 (Black Eyes). As most musicians, especially violinists, prefer playing in 4/4, they always make Gypsy music sound better than Hungarian (ie. more ethnic).

That is why Bartok and Kodaly would often call a piece *Alla Zigeuner,* whereas there is no known example of a piece of Gypsy music called *Alla Bartok.*

Particularly engaging is the Gypsy version of the *Scotch Snap,* as it is called in Scotland, a device often used by Bartok, although not by name because he thought it was a biscuit.

Kodaly is the more ethnic of the two composers because he once used a genuine Gypsy instrument – the cymbalom – in his *Hairy Janos Suite.* The cymbalom is hard to play because the logic behind the string tuning has never been disclosed and because you have to wear a funny costume.

Both Bartok and Kodaly were once offered scholarships by Vaughan Williams to go and study in Norfolk, an offer which they both refused for different reasons.

*Poland*

Polish composers are, in order of importance: Badarzewska, Moniuszko, Rozycki, Bobrzynski and Janiewiecz, all of whom used well-known national dances such as the *Cracovienne,* the *Koniwiak,* the *Kolomyika* and the *Zcyvkroteka.*

All enquiries concerning the above should be addressed to the Polish Cultural Association, c/o Lutos- lawski, 238 King Street, London W6.

*Romania*

Bartok once wrote a *Rumanian Dance* in his *Mikro- kosmos Suite,* but it wasn't a very good one because he got the *Scotch Snap* back to front and didn't know how to spell Romanian.

Romanian music was originally played by bands

Romanian music was originally played by bands of strolling peasants on Grelps – an instrument made of hollowed-out turnips and blown laterally – which never really established itself in the south of the country.

## Scandinavia

Although Scandinavia brought part-singing to Britain, c.1150 (Girlandus Cambrensis), little of note happened after that until 1850, when a tide of national consciousness swept the sub-continent. In Sweden, the operas of Ivar Hallstrom earned him the title of The Swedish Glinka, whilst in spite of being German, Frederic Pacius became known as the Finnish Glinka. Neils Gade nearly became the Danish Glinka, but spoiled it by studying in Leipzig, whereas Valdemar Thrane became the Norwegian Glinka by writing *Fjeldventyret*, for reasons that have not yet become clear.

*Review X*

Write a synopsis of *Kral a Uhlif* and explain why Uhlif behaved as he did.

Spell .............. if you dare, and then try Dargomyszski without looking.

Which overture would you play if you wanted a three-minute egg?

Make sure you spell Romania right.

Was there an Icelandic Glinka and if not, why?

Is Dvorak a Czech or a Slovak? Discuss.

Make a diagram indicating the position of the feet in a Romanian Dance.

What sort of music would you write if you were a Maya?

What would you expect if you asked for a half-pound of Scotch Snaps?

Write a simple tune for a Soprano Grelp in B*b* and then transpose it.

# – Chapter 11 –

## Tchaikovsky

One reason Tchaikovsky was never a member of *The Five* was that he wouldn't let Rimsky-Korsakov finish his pieces for him. Also the group was full up already.

He became the most popular composer in the world in spite of this because of his tunes, of which there were usually four or five good ones per symphony and about 280 per ballet.

Research has recently revealed that these were all at the same tempo: either quarter = 72, eighth = 72, or, in the case of waltzes, dotted half = 72.

This enabled Tchaikovsky to build up a library of Good Tunes, which he could fit into any situation, as and when required.

He had a unique method of cataloguing these, as the following extracts from his diary will show:

IIIa: Plangent. (Oboe) mf *cantabile*.accompaniment: 4 muted horns.length: 6 bars of 6/8, *moderato*.

XVCb: Brutal. (3trbs & tba) fff *marcato*. accompaniment: 4 trpts. length: 3 bars of 4/4, *allegro pesante*.

XXXIX: *Cantando*. Ist & 2nd Violins, mf *cantabile*. 16 bars. accompaniment: harp and string *pizz. Moderato con anima.*

Tchaikovsky used to think up these tunes during his daily two-hour walks and then catalogue them as soon as he got home. It is from details such as these that musicologists can build up a picture of a composer's life that may radically affect future performances of his works.

Thus, the fact that Tchaikovsky was known to trim his beard every Thursday becomes noteworthy only when we take into consideration that it was on a Thursday that he wrote the pizzicato string section in the Scherzo of his *Fourth Symphony*.

The tam-tam stroke in the last movement of the *Sixth* (marked optional) was added only after Tchaikovsky's maid dropped the entire contents of his supper tray on the stairs en route to his work room.

Similarly, the horn fanfares at the beginning of the *Fourth Symphony* were not Fate knocking at the door, but a celebration of the beginning of a long-standing relationship with a lady who insisted on sending him money. This was a good thing in that it provided Tchaikovsky with an income without his having to pretend he was not homosexual.

However, Tchaikovsky and his patroness used to correspond regularly and this appealed greatly to both of them – to his benefactor because she could read about his latest works without having to listen to them, and to Tchaikovsky because some of the ideas he made up in order to have something to write about actually sounded quite good the following morning.

Tchaikovsky's best-known work is the symphonic poem *1812,* which was commissioned by Brock's Fireworks and first performed at the Albert Hall with detonators inside dustbins representing cannon.

The offstage conductor for the first performance was Sir Malcolm Sargent.

Tchaikovsky, himself, preferred *The Dance of the Sugar-plum Fairies,* but composers are notorious for preferring their more récherché works to their popular favorites (c.f. Ravel).

For instance, Tchaikovsky always preferred his *Montenegrin Villagers receiving news of Russia's Declaration of War on Turkey* (1880) to his *Fifth Symphony* because it had more intellectual content.

*Sibelius*

There is no truth in the rumor that Sibelius's *First Symphony* was written by Tchaikovsky, nor that *Tapiola* is a sort of Finnish pudding.

In fact, there is no truth in any gossip about Sibelius, all of which has arisen because no one knew where Finland was except Lenin, and because Sibelius lived in the middle of it, surrounded by brooding forests, lakes, etc.

In spite of the rumors that are bound to gather around a public figure who insists on behaving like a hermit, Sibelius was a kindly man who always regretted that his *First Symphony* ended with two pizzicato string chords.

To the last, he insisted that the horn tune in the finale of his *Fifth Symphony* was not based on *Oh, dry those tears* and that the trumpet was unnecessary at the end of his *Seventh* even though everyone knew that the B-natural couldn't be heard without it.

For most of his life, he was in receipt of a pension from the Finnish government, which shows that when he wrote *Valse Triste* and *Finlandia* it was because he really wanted to.

The English conductor Basil Cameron once went to Finland to ask Sibelius about the existence of his *Eighth Symphony* but he couldn't find him.

Did Sibelius write an *Eighth Symphony* or not? (There is a rumor he finished a fair copy of the score and sent it to the following address: "Basil Cameron Esq. c/o The Savage Club, Royal Albert Hall, London. If lost, please forward to The Garrick Club, Broadcasting House, Whiteladies Road, Bristol, for the attention of the Night Porter."

*Bruckner*

The first thing to remember about Bruckner is that he was not Mahler. The following observations should enable you to clear up this misunderstanding for good:

Mahler could conduct but Bruckner couldn't.

Bruckner was an organist but Mahler wasn't.

Mahler was married and Bruckner wasn't, even though he did write a song called *In April* when he was 44 years old.

Mahler used to enjoy putting grandiose titles at the head of his symphonies, but Bruckner preferred *Number Nine in D minor.*

Mahler was Jewish but Bruckner never was.

Bruckner is mainly admired by serious musicians who understand structure and live in South-East London, whereas Mahler is admired by Jews living in Northwest London who couldn't give a toss about structure. Those who like to see a climax signalled 10 minutes before it arrives are the ones who like Bruckner most.

Bruckner was always secure in the knowledge that what is inevitable is right and vice versa, whereas Mahler could never make up his mind about it.

Bruckner was also fond of Wagner Tubas but Mahler could take them or leave them. On the other hand,

Mahler had an obsession with anvils and wooden boxes with mallets, both of which Bruckner thought vulgar.

Bruckner made of Vienna a small provincial town, whereas Mahler turned it into a world capital. (N.B.: Bruckner once went to Paris to give an organ recital, he said.)

*Review XI*

What tempo would you take a Tchaikovsky tune?

Was Sibelius a rumor and if so who started it?

Give the number of any one of Sibelius's symphonies, but not the *Third*.

Why did Bruckner really go to Paris?

Did Lenin ever meet Sibelius and what would he have said?

How many E*b* chords are there at the end of Sibelius's *Fifth Symphony*?

What was the point of Tchaikovsky's lady friend?

Did Bruckner write *Tales from the Vienna Woods* and if not, why not?

Describe what you usually think about 10 minutes before a Bruckner climax.

Was Mahler essentially a miniaturist?

# – Chapter 12 –

## Germany or Austria? The Final Solution

For almost 200 years these two great countries had been locked in conflict over who was going to be Top Musical Nation. Back and forth the front line swayed, and it was against this background that the two Titans of the late Romantic movement eyed each other, each conscious that it was between the two of them that the final decision was bound to be made.

Gustav Mahler for Austria and Richard Strauss for Germany were born within four years of each other and they were both conductors – by which we mean actually earning a living at it, as opposed to having a go sometimes. Thus began the contest that was to rock the musical world:

"I'm going to double up the brass at the end of *Till Eulenspiegl.*"

"I did that already in my *First Symphony* and I had seven horns to start with."

"I'm using cowbells in my *Alpine Symphony.*"

"I'm using an anvil in my *Eighth.*"

Things like that.

Finally, it was brought home to them that these tactics could only be self-defeating and they arranged to have a secret meeting in Switzerland.

The upshot was a signed and legally witnessed agreement that Strauss would write only tone poems and operas and Mahler would stick to symphonies and song cycles.

There was a leak, of course, and at one point there was even talk of referring them to the Monopolies Commission, but in the end the authorities decided to put the telescope to the blind eye and let the two of them get on with it.

As a result, this undeclared war was watched with fascination by the rest of the musical world. Bets were laid as to which of them would be the next General Music Director of the *Wiener Staatsoper* and or who would finish his next opera (symphony) before the coming November.

It would be pointless to pretend the war was waged with scrupulous honesty. Although Mahler let it be known he wrote only during his summer vacations in the country, he was known to keep a copy of his latest score in the *Dirigentzimmer* at the *Staatsoper* and to be occupied with it when he was supposed to be bowing the string parts of *Salome.*

Nor was Strauss in a position to complain when all Vienna knew that he used to ask some of his better pupils to fill in the woodwind parts for him. Again, it was Strauss who let it be known that *Rosenkavalier* was going to finish with the trio, even though he already had the real ending ready in short score, to be brought out at the second piano rehearsal. Mahler was no less culpable when he added *Urlicht* to his *Second Symphony* three days before the first performance.

Over the years many similar pieces of chicanery were swept under the carpet by one or the other of the two giants, and a final *rapprochement* was only reached in London, which they both hated so passionately that they agreed to sign an armistice if they were both allowed to stay in Vienna for the rest of their lives.

*1894*

This momentous year saw the first performance of *The Afternoon of a Faun* by Debussy, the title of which is so silly that music was never to be the same again. Debussy would have no truck with symphonies or concertos, preferring to write about The Sea, Clouds, Sounds and Perfumes Turning in the Evening Air, etc., etc.

In order not to sound like Wagner, he invented the whole-tone scale and then wrote a music drama about a ring that gets lost in a lake [*Pelleas and Melisande*].

He also wrote *La Mer*, about his mother, and what she did between seven in the morning and midday, about which Ravel was kind enough to say that he particularly liked the bit at a quarter-to-eleven.

Ravel was known as a great wit, and he was always finding ways of making fun of Debussy, who didn't really appreciate it, especially if it was about the whole-tone scale.

Debussy had worked this scale out for himself and he was extremely proud of it. It had one note less than the ordinary major or minor scale and the only place it could modulate to was the whole-tone scale a semitone away from it.

As both scales had only six notes in them, the two together equalled 12, which were all the notes available anyway. If anyone is interested in getting to know more about this fascinating scale, please write to "Deb slash rave dot co slash flop."

It is most important to remember that Debussy is not Ravel and vice versa, and that Ravel was the more brilliant of the two, but less profound because he didn't write *Pelleas and Melisande*.

The fact that he wrote *Bolero* has always been held against him in certain quarters because it is usually played at concerts that already contain *1812* and *Greensleeves*.

Ravel also wrote two operas – one was about teapots and another about clocks – but it should not be thought that he was in any sense a miniaturist. His ballet *Daphnis and Chloe* expanded many of the thoughts Debussy had left out of *L'Apres midi d'un Faun* from an innate sense of propriety.

*The English Renaissance*
*Elgar*

Although Elgar was 37 when Debussy wrote *After-noon of a Faun*, he had not heard of it, and carried on writing as if nothing had happened.

This was typical of a man who lived miles away in Worcestershire and never came up to town. He achieved an international reputation with his *Dream of Geronimo*, an oratorio about the famous Apache chieftain, which he wrote after hearing Coleridge-Taylor's *Hiawatha*.

Elgar did not make Ravel's mistake of being a wit, but he did write a march called *Pomp & Circumstance No. 4,* which had such a well-known tune for its middle section that it achieved immediate national recognition as being as good, if not better, than *God Save the King.*

It was at this point that Elgar did something extremely clever – he arranged for someone to write words to his tune so that it would always be played and sung at events of national importance, such as a war or the *Last Night of the Proms.*

As the words began with the phrase "Land of hope and glory," they were just what was needed to make the English feel better after having been called "the land without music" for the last hundred years.

At the time, no one knew who wrote the words, because Elgar kept it dark, implying that he'd written them himself and therefore should be made Poet Laureate as well as Master of the King's Music.

We are privileged to reveal the name of the real writer for the first time: It was Mr. A.C. Benson.

While he was still a boy, Elgar worked in his father's music shop in Worcester and learnt the trombone and violin.

However, he was an ambitious young man and he managed to overcome these disadvantages in later life by growing a moustache and wearing stiff white collars. Even so, his stature was not really recognized in Germany until Richard Strauss raised his glass "to this great Englishman," and even then not much.

The occasion had been a performance of the *Enigma Variations*, in which each variation was dedicated to a friend of the composer.

It was already a firm favorite in the Home Counties, where people wanted to know who the lady was referred to in the score as "# # #."

It turned out to be Elgar's dog.

Elgar was the quintessential Englishman. He wrote the *Cockaigne Overture* to show he understood the Working Classes, *Falstaff* to show he'd read Shakespeare and *In the South* to show he knew about Italy and the Grand Tour.

Finally, he wrote two symphonies to prove he could, and *The Dream of Gerontius* to show he also believed in God.

He was a totally successful man in all ways – artistically, economically and socially. He even made a success of his marriage.

On the rare occasions when he was hard up, he would turn out pieces like *Salut d'Amour* and *Chanson de Matin* and he managed to make a great success of them as well.

*Delius*

This composer is known as a miniaturist because his two best-known pieces (*On hearing the first Cuckoo in Spring* and *Summer Night on the River*), last only 10 minutes each, if as long.

In spite of that, he also wrote *A Mass of Life*, with words by Nietszche, *Sea Drift* to words by Walt Whitman, six operas, four concertos and 24 works for orchestra, most of which had at least one performance, if not two.

He was a patrician, a free-thinker, a Zarathustran and a man of private means who happened to be born in Bradford. He overcame this disadvantage later by working as an orange grower in Florida and by ending his life in France, where he went blind and died the same year as Elgar, whom he never met.

He greatly enjoyed listening to his own works and talking to Sir Thomas Beecham about them, but to no one else. When he lost his sight, a dedicated young man called Eric Fenby offered to come and stay with him and write down his works for nothing, an offer that Delius accepted with alacrity, and for many years the two of them were to be seen in Delius's garden with Delius saying things like, "Put a dotted minim G on the horn and let it slur across to the flute," to which Fenby would then say "Yes," just like Mozart and Salieri in the film *Amadeus*.

Delius's wife would then come out with tea for them both.

It was, in many ways, an idyllic life.

*Rubbra and Finzi*

These two composers were both very good at writing in the English Pastorale tradition and living in the English countryside. They both owed something, but not much, to Elgar, considerably more to Vaughan Williams and most to R.O.Morris and the young ladies who used to walk up and down Prince Consort Road, outside the Royal College of Music, crying because Sir Edward Bairstow had criticized their counterpoint.

Those were the days when people were just beginning to take English music seriously, at least in England, and any bright lad who could write a tune in the Dorian mode without doubling his octaves was regarded as a serious contender for the crown of Sir Edward Elgar, especially if he lived in the country surrounded by sheep and village pubs.

It was a time when settings of English poets had become really important, a time when half the world was printed in pink and when England was busy throwing down gauntlets at Germany's feet.

These two very English composers were firm friends and they both admired each other's works to the exclusion of almost everyone else.

They both liked living in the country and imbueing themselves with the eternal values of sheep, cows and the English Peasant. Edmund Rubbra also wrote an excellent *Fifth Symphony,* whereas Finzi was a miniaturist who had greatly enjoyed writing *Dies Natalis* and now enjoyed forming various amateur orchestras to play it. His music was thought to have about it a touch of Vaughan Williams but also a touch of Finzi.

He had two good-looking sons who both played string instruments as well as doing other things such as massaging other musicians.

*Review XII*

Whose side are you on – Mahler's or Richard Strauss's? Give one reason why.

Why was Elgar's dog called ###?

Give a personal view on why 1894 was a momentous year for you.

Describe the *Dream of Hiawatha* and its relevance today.

Did Richard Strauss like *Land of Hope and Glory*?

What happened to Debussy's mother at a quarter-to-eleven?

Did Elgar mean anything to Cardinal Newman?

Why do you think that Ravel was less profound than Debussy? Give two examples.

Write the libretto for an opera about teapots.

Write a biography of Delius, Rubbra and Finzi, making it clear which was which.

## – Chapter 13 –

*Modern Music*

This began, as we have seen, in 1894 and it is still with us today. In fact, it may be still with us in 2025, unless this book is a long time going to press in which case it may not.

We have divided the subject into Sub-headings to increase the confusion.

*The Dodecaphonics*

These were originally all Germans, because Germany was upset at the French behaving in such a high-handed way when they invented the Whole-tone scale, despite the fact that they knew it was really Germany's responsibility.

They were also upset at having lost the First World War, and because of this, they got hold of a man called Zemlinsky, who was teaching Schoenberg at the time, and told him to start a new school of composition.

This Zemlinsky achieved by saying to Schoenberg 'Are you a Democrat?' to which Schoenberg replied 'Yes.' 'Then you must never write anything that does not respect the democratic principle. All notes have equal rights and must have equal opportunities. Therefore, when you have written a note, you must never write it again until all the other notes have also had a turn.'

'OK,' said Schoenberg. 'You're the boss – if that's what you want, I won't fight it.'

Nor did he.

He was quick to see that Debussy's two whole-tone scales equalled one chromatic scale when put together, which was what he'd been using all the time, especially in his most recent composition, *The Guru-lieder.*

However, he'd been feeling lately that this chromatic scale was allowing him too much freedom because it seemed to be taking him so long to decide between one note and another. Often, he would sit for hours thinking 'F sharp or G?' until his wife would come in with a small glass of schnapps and say 'Dinner in five minutes, liebling' or words to that effect.

Then, when they were sitting at table, she would say, 'Why is your dearest brow furrowed?' in German, and he would say, also in German: 'I can't decide between F sharp and G.' Whereupon, Mrs. Schoenberg would put down her knife and fork with great decision and say, 'Liebling – you need a system. How can important decisions like these be left to chance?'

'Just what Zemlinsky said', replied Schoenberg, and the matter was settled.

By the time he had eaten his Schokolade-Nuss-Palichinka he was back at his piano, putting Zemlinsky's dictum into effect and almost immediately he found himself writing with less freedom.

In due course, as his reputation increased, he began having pupils of his own and to these he taught his new method until it became developed into a fully-fledged System.

By now, Schoenberg's music was beginning to get pretty dense because, if he'd just written a 'C' and he wanted to write another one almost immediately, it meant he would have to find places for all the other eleven notes first. Sometimes he'd chuck them in all over the place just to get rid of them.

Nevertheless, it was in this way that Schoenberg became a formulative influence on modern music after the war that Germany lost, which was exactly what the Germans had had in mind.

Anyone who refused to use Schoenberg's system was labelled Reactionary and wasn't listened to very seriously, whilst anyone who kept on writing like Vaughan Williams weren't listened to at all, except by Vaughan Williams himself, who hadn't heard what it was all about because he was getting a bit deaf.

In order to capitalize on this victory, the Germans (and Austrians) let it be known that no composers would be eligible for Government Grants if they had not yet mastered the new system, and this meant going to Schoenberg for lessons.

'There, Liebling,' Mrs. Schoenberg used to say as she went out to buy her bottles of Doppelt-Korn and caviare. 'See how things have picked up since you invented your system.'

Schoenberg was also pleased, so he would pat her in a friendly way as he made his way into his studio where one of his new pupils awaited him. Although he now had a schedule of fifteen pupils per day, two things concerned him. One was that only two of them were any good and the other was that he didn't seem to have the time to write his own music any more.

'Never mind, Liebling,' Mrs. Schoenberg would say, 'Think how many pupils you now have who can do it for you.'

At which, Schoenberg shook his head sadly and went into his studio to teach another.

This one was Anton Webern, a dedicated Dodecaphonic who believed that people could only listen to two notes at a time and only concentrate for about three minutes. Although he was probably right, this never made him a really popular composer.

Schoenberg used to try to move him from this stance: 'Think of the People, Anton,' he would say. 'It is for them that you are writing. It is your job to convert them towards higher thoughts – with your music you can turn them into good citizens, into people with high moral codes and vaulting ambitions.'

'No, it isn't,' said Webern, and that was that.

Schoenberg's other talented pupil was Alban Berg, who cared so much about his fellow human-beings that he spent most of his life writing two Operas: the first one *Wozzeck* was about a man tormented to death by a cruel world, and the second *Lulu* was about a woman in a similar situation.

'Go into the world,' said Schoenberg. 'Show them all how to live useful lives, how to work for the greater good of Mankind, how to make our world a better place to live in.'

'OK,' said Berg, thinking about knives, blood and moonlight.

He was an Expressionist who tried to portray life around him as it was lived. He was happily married and lived quietly in Vienna as a teacher.

*The Folk-song Revival*

In England this started as an off-shoot of the Ramblers' Association until the Royal College of Music agreed to accept it as a Dictation Test. Eventually it became quite a thriving industry and there was scarcely a farmer in Norfolk who could not toss off a tune for the price of a pint.

The industry also gave rise to what was jocularly known as 'The-Same-Old-Cow-looking-over-the-Same-Old-Gate' school of composition, in which Vaughan Williams played the part of the gate. Their headquarters were, of course, at the Royal College of Music and the London-and-North-Eastern Railway used to offer them special cheap-rate Group Tickets to Norfolk and back.

As you will remember there was also a Folk-song Revival in Hungary developed by Bartok and Kodaly, who got all the peasants to sing their folk-songs in unison. This was said to be an awe-inspiring sound and was much admired by the monks at Solesme, who were still going strong.

Urban folk-songs were largely the business of the Workers' Music Association in Bayswater who were responsible for publishing and recording a number of ethnic songs about Marshall Tito, the McCarthy trials, the Siege of Leningrad and the coal-miners of Barnsley.

The latter came under the special heading of Work-songs like *The Tarriers' Rant* and *Bring up Danny's body from the Coal-face, Mother.*

They could be loosely described as politically aware and were largely responsible for things like Left-wing Summer Schools and Alan Bush.

Gradually, the Left-wing Folk-song movement came to include any songs about social deprivation, whether they were Sea-Shanties, Ploughing-songs or Guerilla songs. Small groups of singers from the WMA used to make themselves available to sing at Communist Party rallies or Wholesale Co-operative Society raffles and occasionally they would put on a concert at St. Pancras Town Hall with a real orchestra of Left-wing professionals who would agree to give back their fees to the Working-Class movement.

Those were the days when the USSR had opened the second Front and were thus our Allies, so the British Establishment had no excuse for stopping the WMA from giving concerts about how wonderful Stalin was. They did, however, successfully scupper the career of Alan Bush, who kept on writing music of social relevance well into the seventies as if nothing had happened.

*Further Reactions to the Romantic Tradition*

Finding an unwanted freedom thrust upon them by the break-up of the classic and romantic tradition, composers all over Europe tried to find ways of getting rid of it, rather as Schoenberg had in Germany.

These were composers of a younger generation and not only was the First World War over, but the Second had not quite begun.

Perhaps two of the most successful were Hindemith and Milhaud. Hindemith's method was to pick a note – any note – and then say, 'This is a Root'. At which point, he would subject it to intense scrutiny and tell you which other notes in the scale were good and which were rotten.

He did this by a cunning use of the Harmonic Series. Once he had picked his note and called it a Root, he then wrote down the Harmonic series based on that Root. In other words, he would say to himself and to anyone else who happened to be listening: 'If this note is a Root, then its first harmonic should be an octave which is a Good Note. The second should be a Fifth, which is also fairly good, but the third sounds out-of-tune and is definately a Bad Note. And so on up the Harmonic Series. Ganz Einfach when you've grasped the principle.'

However, Hindemith also had a lot of other prin-
ciples. One was that music was no use if there was no-
one there to hear it and also that it was a composer's
job to write lots of stuff for beginners so that they could
learn to play better. Thus Hindemith's music nearly
always had a purpose, and these purposes combined
with his theories about Good and Rotten Notes meant
that his music always sounded so clean and and healthy
that they called it 'Bread-and-Butter Music' and said
that no-one must produce any unless there was someone around to play it, eat it or listen to it.

In the end, Schoenberg had to confess, with some
reluctance, that Hindemith's music was a good thing
because it actually did more to move the Citizens of the
World towards a better and more useful life than either
Berg or Webern. Hindemith also earned a living playing the viola in a string quartet. 'The Viola!' said Schoenberg sourly, when he heard about it. 'Middle Parts!'

Meanwhile, in France, Darius Milhaud found a sim-
pler but equally effective solution to the problem of what
to do now that the Classical Tradition was a thing of the
past.

What Milhaud had always done best was to write
French Chansons like Roland and Maurice Chevalier,
but as everyone laughed at him when he did, he decided
to write half-a-dozen of them, all in different keys, and
then play them together. So piquant was the effect that
no lesser a man than Jean Cocteau said, 'You have
invented Polytonality and you can now be a member of
my Group'.

Milhaud found this method of writing so satisfying
that he stayed with it for the rest of his life.

*Les Six*

With *Les Six*, the French were taking a leaf out of the Russian book [see *The Five*] instead of the other way round, which had usually been the case in the past.

The composers who decided to form this group [pronounced Lay Cease) were George Auric, Louis Durey, Arthur Honneger, Darius Milhaud, Francis Poulenc and Germaine Tailleferre [as the only woman in the group and as Feminism had not yet set in, she usually served the tea and *petit-fours*].

These people all banded together so they could write the sort of music they liked without being attacked on street corners by aggresive groups of Dodecaphonics, often bussed in especially from Germany. In other words, it was a defensive alliance.

What sort of music did they want to write?

They wanted to find music that reflected all those things that were typically French, such as bars, nightclubs, the Moulin Rouge, Montmartre, Montparnasse, *Les Deux Magots*, the Left Bank and Student Riots, so they thought up a lot of innocuous cafe tunes and tarted them up with a few wrong notes and the occasional funny instrument so that they didn't sound like innocuous cafe tunes any more. Instead, they sounded like Lay Cease making fun of innocuous café tunes whilst laughing, smoking and drinking absinthe if they could find any.

As we have seen, in Milhaud's case this led him to write in several different keys at once and call it polytonality, but the others weren't as serious as Milhaud, so for them it was enough if they wrote out a bit of café music and then changed all the bass notes by a semitone.

The audiences loved it. This was contemporary music without tears. George Auric became a top film music composer, Francis Poulenc wrote songs for Pierre Bernac to sing, Honneger wrote music about steam trains, Milhaud wrote movingly about The Creation of the World and Germaine Tailleferre, as always, made the tea.

Little is known about Louis Durey except that he once wrote a passacaglia in which the theme was a tone higher than the other parts. Lay Cease ceased with the advent of World War II and the end of civilization as we know it.

*Review XIII*

Repeat one note of a Twelve-tone Scale without anyone noticing.

Does Alban Berg strike you as a nice person?

Revive a folksong without using artificial respiration.

Why was Hindemith called the "Telemann of the 20th-century" and if not, why not?

Describe Polytonality, if you dare.

Write a work song for the knitting-women of the French Revolution.

Is *The Tarriers Rant* a song or a complaint?

Why was Stravinsky never a member of Lay Cease?

Did you ever join the Workers' Music Association? If so, please enclose your name, passport number and one photograph.

# – Chapter 14 –

*Stravinsky*

Stravinsky started by sounding like Rimsky-Korsakov (The Firebird) and ended up sounding like Webern (Abraham and Isaac).

In between, he sounded like Bach, Tchaikovsky, Pergolesi, Gluck, Duke Ellington, Schubert and Stravinsky – especially the latter.

At one time, Stravinsky suffered from people saying he hadn't got a style, whereas what they meant was he had too many. Couldn't he decide on one and then stick to it?

Was he one of the world's butterflies, taking a sip from this flower and then on to the next? Not only were all his styles eclectic, but he made a song and dance about them by saying things like "After Pergolesi," "In homage to Gluck," or "Dedicated to the Glory of God and the Boston Symphony Orchestra."

In the end, people began to realize it wasn't so much that he sounded like all the others as that they all seemed to end up sounding like him. It is noteworthy that he never tried to sound like Hindemith or Milhaud.

When he had finished *The Rite of Spring*, Stravinsky's methods changed. Instead of writing big crunchy chords for hundreds of instruments, he decided to become economical and straightforward.

He would sit down at 10 o'clock in the morning and write until one, by which time he would have committed about half-a-dozen bars to paper. These he would then throw away before lunch – usually a little Bortsch and rye bread – in order to start all over again afterwards.

At four, he would have a small cup of Russian tea and a *Petit Beurre* and throw out a few more. By the time dinner was ready, he would have a vodka and a spoonful of Beluga caviar first and then review the day's work. Four or five notes he might decide would be OK for the following morning – the rest he would put carefully in the wastepaper basket.

Among the many words of advice he passed on to future generations of composers was the aphorism: "Be mean with your notes!"

If someone said, "What about the *Rite of Spring*?" he would smile and say, "Everyone is allowed their adolescence," and then light another Balkan Sobranie.

### Social Realism

Social Realism was invented by Lenin and Trotsky to give musicians something to do in the Revolution. So successful was this idea that from then on, the State had its work cut out building enough dams, factories, steel mills and collectives to keep up with the stream of works commemorating them.

In the end, the State had to announce that half the works it was receiving were no good in order to give the manufacturing base a chance to catch up.

It was at this point the State made a fatal mistake, by inviting Prokofiev to come back to Russia from Paris.

To their surprise, Prokofiev agreed and immediately began producing more and more commemorative works because he thought that was what they wanted. The trouble was that this time the State couldn't say the works were no good because they were by Prokofiev.

In the end, they decided to take it out on Shostakovich, who was younger and hadn't been to Paris.

Again, however, they were hoist by their own petard.

As soon as they started telling Shostakovich the music he was writing nowadays wasn't any good, he started apologizing and then began again writing a series of very long symphonies commemorating the various revolutions in which the Russian Communist Party had been involved.

So long were these works that the cost of copying the parts and rehearsing them almost bankrupted the Union of Soviet Composers so that, in the end, they were forced to ask him to stop. Unfortunately, this coincided with Shostakovitch discovering that the opening initials of his name (DSCH) made a tune. So pleased was he with this discovery that he at once began writing a whole lot more works based on his initials, culminating in the immensely long *Tenth Symphony*.

Something had to be done, the State realized, to stem this flow of works, so they persuaded the Union of Soviet Composers to accuse Shostakovitch of perpetuating the Cult of the Individual, which meant that none of his DSCH works could be played.

As soon as Shostakovitch heard of this decision, he said that DSCH was nothing to do with his name but meant "Don't Sacrifice Our Childrens' Hospitals," whereupon the State found itself again thwarted and had a long, serious talk with Shostakovitch, at the end of which he promised in future to write only shortish pieces for smallish orchestras and/or string quartets.

So honor was, to some extent, satisfied.

It was later calculated that the energy of Soviet composers in turning out commemorative works ahead of schedule contributed more to the industrialization of the USSR than any other single factor.

*America*

For 200 years, Americans had been trying to find a National Style and the nearest they'd got to it was Charles Ives, who was an insurance agent.

However, living in New York at the time there was a harmony teacher called Rubin Goldmark and amongst his many pupils were George Gershwin and Aaron Copland.

Gershwin was not much worried about finding an American Style – all he wanted to do was to write a piece with clarinet glissandos in it for Paul Whiteman's Band, so he wrote *A Rhapsody in Blue* and then took a boat to Paris to study orchestration with Ravel.

This gave him the idea that perhaps he should write a piece about an American in Paris and maybe put in some of the car horns that seemed to be such a feature of Parisian life, so he went to a cycle shop and bought four of them and then asked Ravel how best to incorporate them into his composition. While he was waiting, he put in a long tune for jazz trumpet and then submitted the whole to the 1931 Jury of the International Festival of New Music who, somewhat surprisingly, agreed to play it.

That year, the Festival was being held in London, but as none of the critics much liked *An American in Paris*, Gershwin returned to New York and decided to write an opera.

That was the beginning of *Porgy and Bess*, and while he was waiting for someone to produce it, he wrote a *Cuban Overture,* some *Jazz Piano Preludes* and about 10 successful musicals.

Then he died, and it was decided he had done more to create an American style than anyone else, even if he hadn't meant to.

The person who did mean to, however, was Aaron Copland, and he determined that he was going to be the first person to find the solution. So he also went to Paris, although not to Ravel but to Nadia Boulanger, who was a specialist in this sort of thing.

"Very well," she said, "We will examine the situation. What in your opinion, is typically American?"

Copland was going to say "Hot dogs," but he changed his mind, and after some thought, he said: "The Midwest ... the Prairies."

"What is Prairies?" demanded Boulanger.

Copland explained.

"Ah, *je comprend tous*. Central Asia. Borodin had similar problems. It is the Fifth for which we seek – the open, bare Fifth. Go away and write."

So Copland went away and wrote *Billy the Kid* and when he showed it to Boulanger she recognized it immediately.

"We have – what shall we say? – cracked it. Together we have made the American Style. We will now have a cup of tea."

At this, Copland returned to America and began writing a series of works about the Midwest, all based on the fifth, which established him as America's No. 1 stylist.

Perhaps the climax of his early career came when the famous chiropodist, Martha Graham, asked him to write the score for a ballet she had in mind about the Appalachian Mountains and the early pioneer stock in Pennsylvania.

This was so exactly up Copland's alley that he at once asked Mrs. Sprague Coolidge if she could afford to give him the money to write it. As a result, he based part of the work on a folk-song called *The Gift that was Simple*, which was Copland's way of saying a big thank you to Mrs. Sprague Coolidge.

Copland's example led to large numbers of young Americans setting to and writing about their own country, sometimes by producing "Hoe-downs," sometimes by trying to beat Honneger at his own game with engine pieces like *Pennsylvania 2847 crossing the Midwest Badlands* and less often with urban numbers like *Room 23a on Second Floor Front at Sundown*. The covers of these scores were usually reproductions of paintings by Hopper and although the fifth always remained very much in evidence, the younger composers also began branching out into more urban intervals like the augmented fourth and the major second. Nor was the rhythmic element neglected, often taking the form of decorations on woodblocks.

Two exceptions to the above tendencies were Samuel Barber and a New York Italian called Gian-Carlo Menotti, now living in Edinburgh.

Both these composers were thorough-going Romantics who cared not a jot for the Prairies or Pennsylvania 2847, nor could they give a damn about the fifth if you gave some away free with packets of popcorn.

These composers were 20th-century Romantics writing in the styles inherited from their forefathers: in Menotti's case, Verdi and Puccini, and in Barber's, Brahms.

They each had their immediate successes – Barber with his *Adagio for Strings* from his *String Quartet* and Menotti with his Kafkaesque opera, *The Consul*, which was so popular that it ran in London for three weeks. This was a great achievement, bearing in mind that *Dido and Aeneas* ran for only one night.

Younger than either Barber or Menotti was Leonard Bernstein, who decided to share styles with Stravinsky rather than with Copland, much to Mde. Boulanger's disgust.

Where Copland was Appalachian Rural, Bernstein became New York Urban and began writing pieces about Times Square and Coney Island.

There was no doubt that music in America was by now beginning to buzz with creativity – Harry Partch was building orchestras out of goldfish bowls, George Antheil was scoring pieces for aeroplane propellers and Ives was seeing how far away from each other two orchestras could sit before they had to stop.

Then came all the European composers (see next chapter) who were chucked out by the Nazis and who thought that maybe they would like it better in America.

*Social Criticism: Berlin in the '30s*

Berlin was a very tough, nasty place full of rich, fat old men going to dirty nightclubs and touching pretty young girls, and a group of artists such as George Gross, Berthold Breckt and Kurt Vile decided to show it up for what it was, namely a place full of rich, fat old men going to dirty nightclubs, etc.

To do this, Kurt Vile wrote some very catchy cabaret numbers and then put nasty harmonies underneath them to show how he felt.

As a result of this and because he was Jewish, Hitler made him leave Germany and go to America, where he wrote a lot more catchy cabaret numbers with nice harmonies underneath to show how much he liked it there.

However, when Senator Joe McCarthy began holding some witch-hunts to find out who were Reds and who weren't, everyone began liking it a bit less.

Perhaps Vile's biggest successes were the songs he wrote for *The Threepenny Opera*, a piece based on John Gay's *Beggars' Opera*. In this, Gay created a vivid sketch of life among the London rich in the 18th century, which Breckt and Vile brilliantly transposed into the Berlin rich in the 20th without sacrificing any of Gay's principal preoccupations.

So far, we have said little about George Gross. That is because he was a painter and this is a book about music.

### Canada

Not all the Jews went to America, nor was America the only place that was getting worried about finding a Style.

The trouble is that it wasn't Canada either because the Canadians weren't worried about that sort of thing. They figured that if America had found one, that would do fine for them as well, and that if the Jewish immigrants hadn't found one by the time they got as far as Canada, they never would.

In any case, why should they start worrying about style when they'd been worrying about the French since 1663? In fact, they were world experts in worrying.

The French-Canadians were worried about the English; the English-Canadians were worried about the French; the Ukrainians were worried about the Church and the Communists and the Amerindians were worried about everyone. There was a Scottish problem, a Chinese problem, a U.S. problem and then there were the Jews.

These problems all boiled down to who was there first.

Unfortunately, the English and the French both thought it was them, so in the end they made a decision to share the best bits of Canada between themselves and insist that they each spoke each other's language. That meant that all the French spoke English and all the English spoke French. Ha-ha.

From the start, music, although officially an international language – *une langue internationale* – was regarded as either French or English, by which is meant it was either the Montreal Symphony with Claude Champagne being Faure or the Toronto Symphony with Healey Willan being Vaughan Williams.

Shortly after this, all the other towns began forming orchestras: the Halifax Symphony, the Winnipeg Symphony, the Saskatoon Symphony, the Edmonton Symphony, the Calgary Philharmonic and the Vancouver Symphony.

It was like you weren't civilized if you didn't have a Symphony Orchestra, and if you had a Symphony Orchestra you weren't civilised if you didn't have a University as well, and Universities meant professors and professors meant composers.

There happened to be a great deal of nothing much in between each of these different centres, so that composers began being classed as Winnipeg composers or Edmonton composers or Montreal or Toronto composers, and to play them anywhere else became an act bordering on infidelity.

The shadow of Hindemith hung heavily over Canadian music for about 50 years, but later the younger generation became quick to pick up some of the labor-saving devices that were being joyfully exploited by their European colleagues.

*Britain between the Wars*
*The Renegades*

Sadly, there were some British composers who did not subscribe to the Folkmusic Revival but laid themselves open to foreign influences, even to the extent of going abroad.

This had a regrettable effect on various other composers who had very properly stayed at home, but before British music could be sucked into a dangerous morass of eclecticism, the Second World War intervened and they all went off to join the Pioneer Corps or the Guards' Bands.

105

1812 And all That

*Military Bands*

It would be regrettable if note were not made at this juncture of the honorable place taken by the military band in the symphonic repertoire, for there is no better way of drowning a symphony orchestra and a choir of 2,000 than by adding a military band at the appropriate moment. No one knew this better than Sir William Walton when he placed several of them a couple of miles away for *Belshazzar's Feast*. All the more surprising is it, therefore, that Berlioz should have written a piece for military bands (*Symphonie funebre et triomphale*) and added strings later. Surely the master of orchestration knew they would make no difference.

A surer touch is demonstrated by Sir Malcolm Arnold in his *United Nations Cantata*, in which the military bands [in full marching order] make their entrances at different times from different areas of the hall. The dramatic effect of this *coup de theatre* is enhanced if busbies are worn.

*Review XIV*

Write a short piece of Stravinsky in the style of Tchaikovsky.

Could you commemorate a steel mill ahead of schedule if you tried?

Name one person who was in Paris in 1930.

Did Christopher Isherwood write *Mack the Knife*?

Spell Kurt Vile.

What artistic benefits did insurance agents bring to America?

What sort of tea did Nadia Boulanger drink?

Was Martha Graham a chiropodist or a chorologist?

Was Aaron Copland really simple?

Write an opera in the style of Menotti so that it will run for three weeks without stopping.

Write a National Anthem for the country of your choice.

Name some of the Glasses that Harry Partch invented.

Which of the Guards Bands are best and why?

# – Chapter 15 –

*Post-war Re-appraisals*

The most important of these were that Britten and Shostakovich had become great composers – Britten by starting the Aldeburgh Festival and Shostakovich by realizing that his initials made a tune.

Other Re-appraisals were:

1. That Bartok should have stayed in Hungary.
2. That Stravinsky was great after all.
3. That no one had given enough thought to Janacek.
4. That Hindemith was a bit of a bore, really.
5. That someone called Nielsen wrote symphonies.
6. That the British Renegades (Walton, Tippett, Berkeley, Fricker, Searle, Rawsthrone et al) didn't have to write folksongs if they didn't want to.
7. That England was no longer *Das Lande ohne Musik*. Hooray.
8. Which was?

*The British Renegades*

These were the British composers who grew up between the wars and may even have studied at the Royal College of Music but who cleverly avoided the folksong Revivalists by using different pubs.

Sir William Walton, as he was known, studied music at Oxford and also with an ancient family called the Sitwells, who turned him into a thoroughly civilized young man with a wide knowledge of all the arts.

Nevertheless, the fact that he was born in Oldham may have been something of a disadvantage to his career because when he wrote accompaniments to some of Edith Sitwell's poems in 1923, they made him speak them into a megaphone with a mask over his face.

He followed this with an overture called *Portsmouth Point*, which was based on some thoroughly disgraceful drawings by Thomas Rowlandson.

In due course he wrote *Belshazzar's Feast*, an extremely loud choral work in which people kept shouting *"Mene, mene tekel Upharsin"* for as long as possible. Lord Berners, to whom the work was dedicated, was said to be in two minds about it.

It has been fashionable to link together the names of Lennox Berkeley and Benjamin Britten merely because they shared a windmill in Suffolk when they were young. But in fact that was all they had in common.

Lennox Berkeley was more French than Britten, having studied in Paris with Guess-Who instead of staying decently at the Royal College of Music with Frank Bridge.

At first, it seemed pretty obvious that Berkeley was the best, and when Britten went to America to write the *Sinfonia da Requiem* that had been commissioned by the Emperor of Japan – the same one who had commissioned the Pearl Harbour incident – it seemed even more obvious.

It was not to be.

As soon as Britten got back to England and settled in Aldeburgh, not far from his previous windmill, he wrote *Peter Grimes*, the opera that had everything – rough seamen in a closed community rubbing shoulders with middle-class school-mistresses, social commentary and a young apprentice who got drowned. It even had a fugue, a passacaglia and Peter Pears.

It was an instant success, and Britten never looked back in anger again, something he had been wont to do once or twice before. Even the Germans had to admit that they were beaten.

Naturally, there were also a lot of not quite brilliant enough young composers waiting somewhat disconsolately in the wings, all waiting to do their bit towards consolidating Britain's new No. 1 status. It wasn't going to be easy, but by making them take scholarships in France, Manchester and the USA, it was felt that a generation might soon be put together that would be worthy successors of Great Britten.

*Review XV*

Have you given enough thought to Janacek?

What have you ever been mean with?

Which of Stravinsky's styles do you like the best?

Did Britten and Jean Francaix have an *Entente Cordiale?* Why not?

Was Britten thinking of the Emperor of Japan when he wrote his *Sinfonia da Requiem?*

Can you spell what the choirs shouted in *Belshazzar's Feast?*

Were the works of Sir Malcolm Arnold not included in this section because they were too popular?

# – Chapter 16 –

*Post-war Discoveries*
*Electronic Music*

This was the most important French discovery since Roland and it was known as *Musique Concrete* because it had its first studio in a high-rise on the wrong side of Montparnasse.

Its first director – Pierre to his friends – was sponsored by ORTF, which was French for BBC. For some reason, the French believed that all its sound sources should be naturalistic – a train crashing or a cow farting – and it was one of its tenets that the music itself should come from the manipulation of this source material.

In contradistinction, the Deutsche Hydro-Electric Studio in Hamburg insisted that all its source material should be electronically produced "white-sound" and it was from these that Karlheinz Stockhausen produced his three-day epics for 24 orchestras that were to become so successful in Germany, especially Hamburg.

Britain's contribution to the new art form was the establishment of the BBC Radiophonic Workshop, which achieved an enviable reputation under its director, Dr. Who.

Since those early days, electronic music has found its way into the bulk of the contemporary orchestral repertoire. This means that lots of live players playing live instruments are failing to find work whereas the firms that transport electronic equipment are finding a good deal.

A precurser of *Musique Concrete* was an electric keyboard instrument called the Ondes Martinot, which could imitate the sound of most instruments with uncanny accuracy. It is, therefore, odd that it has never been engaged to play a classical concerto.

Messiaen used the instrument in his *Turangalila Symphony*, where its unearthly sounds contributed greatly to the unearthly sounds of the whole.

### That Titles Matter

This liberating discovery was made by Universal Edition and its success soon spread to most other publishing houses in Europe and the Far East.

Gone were the days of *Symphony No. IV in F-sharp minor* and in came titles like *Miss Donnithorne's Maggot*, *ST/48-016240183* and *Over Her Shoulder I Could See All Their Poor Faces Looking Down at Me.*

Occasionally someone would produce a piece with a relatively straightforward title such as *Music for a Cold Night* or *Two Ideas looking for an Orchestra* but everyone had begun to realize that *Piano Concerto in C minor* was no longer good enough.

Nor were posters that merely said:
"London Symphony Orchestra
Festival Hall, June 3rd at 7.30.
Beethoven"
These were now replaced by:
"Ashkenazy plays Tchaikovsky"
or "Bernstein and Mahler – the Two Titans"
or "Mainly Mozart"
or "Stravinsky's Greatest Hit – *The Rite*"

### Aleatoric Music

This means "Make it up as you go along" and it was developed initially as a reaction to Boulez' *Le Marteau sans Maitre* [The Doorknocker without a Master], which was so complicated that no one could follow it without a score, let alone with one.

It thus needed only a small leap of the imagination to realize that if you wrote "Rush about all over the instrument for 30 seconds," the result would be much the same as *Marteau* for a fraction of the effort.

Later on, subtleties were introduced, such as: "Rush about all over the instrument like a pear glistening" or "Draw a map of Iceland using the 5 notes indicated."

This sort of writing had a number of predictable consequencies.

For the executant, it was preferable to learning how to play impossibly difficult passages or read complicated rhythms with rapidly changing time signatures. On the other hand, the embarrassment caused by performing tricks like these on their instruments stayed with some musicians for the rest of their lives.

As far as can be ascertained, no instrumentalists have so far made any claims on the Performing Rights Society for their inventions.

Other labor-saving devices that have been discovered are:

*Unpitched Percussion*

Given enough players and instruments, this has been found to be a fairly satisfactory way of filling in the odd 20 minutes during a symphony without having recourse to real music.

*Electronic Tapes*

One advantage of this is called "Tape Delay," which means that players can hear their mistakes just after they've made them.

*Minimalism*

This is by far the greatest discovery of the 20th century, because four bars of anything, repeated endlessly, can induce a state of hypnosis in which all critical faculties are suspended. Works can be as long or as short as you like – usually as long – and rehearsal time is kept down to the minimum.

*The Future*

Stylistically, music has come full circle since 1894. It has survived, if that is the word, the stringent rules of the Twelve Toners, the slightly less stringent rules of Hindemith's *Gebrauchsmusik*, the Dada-ism of the "Wrong-note School" and the cosiness of the Folksong Revivalists.

People now write eclectically, in any style that suits them. The battles of the past have been fought and no one seems either better or worse for them. Critical opinion is no longer concerned with Style – a work can be weak or strong but never wrong.

Even pieces that do virtually nothing for half-an-hour except play some extremely slow chords are not dismissed.

Nor should it be assumed that String Quartets, Symphony Orchestras, Choirs and Piano Recitals and other more traditional ensembles are becoming merely the Custodians of a Museum Art.

On the contrary, they are trying desperately not to become Custodians of a Museum Art. It's only that it takes so much time and costs so much.

*Review XVI*

Write four bars that might induce hypnosis.

Make up a good title and send it to a composer.

Compose a work for symphony orchestra and subject it to tape delay.

Produce some Museum Art and then find a building for it.

*Review XVI* continued

Think of a labor-saving device.

What is the future of electronic music in 300 words?

Could you play the Dvorak *Cello Concerto* on an Ondes Martinot? Why?

Rush about all over your instrument for 20 minutes and then put it away and go home.

Pour yourself a large scotch and soda.

# – Index –

# – About the Author –

At 16, Lawrence Leonard was playing the cello in the London Symphony Orchestra under Sir Henry Wood and during the following years he was fortunate enough to play under Richard Strauss, Clemens Krauss, Joseph Krips, Leopold Stokowsky and John Barbirolli.

At 21 he began studying conducting himself, privately with Ernest Ansermet and Erich Kleiber and in Paris with Jean Fournet. His first professional appointment was as Associate Conductor with the BBC Northern Orchestra, followed by five years as Barbirolli's Assistant-Conductor with the Halle.

He premiered *West Side Story* in London and conducted opera and concerts with major orchestras throughout Europe, Japan, Scandinavia and Canada, where he was Music Director of the Edmonton Symphony for five years.

In 1989 a heart attack led to Lawrence Leonard developing a second career as a writer and composer. His orchestration for piano and orchestra of Mussorgsky's *Pictures at a Exibition* has been recorded by the Philharmonia, and his tone poem *Mezoon,* by the Royal Philharmonic. His first novel (for children) was published at this time. Since then he has written another two novels and five full-length plays.

Emma Bebbington has been influenced from an early age by British illustrators Carl Giles and Norman Thelwell. She is currently studying fine art at Falmouth College of Arts in Cornwall. Her other interests are playing the guitar and piano. This is her first publishing endeavour.

*1812 And all That*
© Lawrence Leonard, 2000
© Emma Bebbington (Cartoons), 2000

First published in Canada by
Sound AndVision
359 Riverdale Avenue
Toronto, Canada M4J 1A4
*http://www.soundandvision.com*
E-mail: musicbooks@soundandvision.com

First printing, October 2000
1 3 5 7 9 11 13 15 - printing - 14 12 10 8 6 4 2

---

*Canadian Cataloguing in Publication Data*
Leonard, Lawrence
1812 and all that: a concise history of music
from 30.000 BC to the millennium
Includes index
isbn 0-920151-33-7
1. Music – History and criticism – Humor. I.
Bebbington, Emma, 1978- . II. Title
ML160.L582 2000      780'.207      C00-931811-9

---

Cover design by Jim Stubbington
Typeset in Bookman Old Style
Printed and bound in Canada

I Wanna Be Sedated
*Pop Music in the Seventies*
by Phil Dellio & Scott Woods
cartoons by Dave Prothero
preface by Chuck Eddy
isbn 0-920151-16-7

Love Lives of the Great Composers
*From Gesualdo to Wagner*
by Basil Howitt
isbn 0-920151-18-3

How to Stay Awake
*During Anybody's Second Movement*
by David E. Walden
cartoons by Mike Duncan
preface by Charlie Farquharson
isbn 0-920151-20-5

A Working Musician's Joke Book
by Daniel G. Theaker
cartoons by Mike Freen
preface by David W. Barber
isbn 0-920151-23-X

The Composers
*A Hystery of Music*
by Kevin Reeves
preface by Daniel Taylor
isbn 0-920151-29-9

How To Listen To Modern Music
*Without Earplugs*
by David E. Walden
cartoons by Mike Duncan
foreword by Bramwell Tovey
isbn 0-920151-31-0

The Thing I've Played With the Most
*Professor Anthon E. Darling Discusses*
*His Favourite Instrument*
by David E. Walden
cartoons by Mike Duncan
isbn 0-920151-35-3

## A Note from the Publisher

Sound And Vision books may be purchased for educational or promotional use or for special sales. If you have any comments on this book or any other book we publish or if you would like a catalogue, please write to us at: Sound And Vision, 359 Riverdale Avenue, Toronto, Canada M4J 1A4.

Or visit our website at: www.soundandvision.com. We would really like to hear from you.

We are always looking for original books to publish. If you have an idea or manuscript that is in the genre of *musical humour* including educational themes, please contact us at our address. Thank you for purchasing or borrowing this book.

Geoffrey Savage
*Publisher*

Watch out for the opening of www.musicalstuff.com in the new year.